THE KNOWLEDGE
MOST WORTH HAVING

T0373369

A publication of the Seventy-fifth Anniversary Year
of THE UNIVERSITY OF CHICAGO

THE KNOWLEDGE
MOST WORTH HAVING

Edited by Wayne C. Booth

THE UNIVERSITY OF CHICAGO PRESS
Chicago & London

THE UNIVERSITY OF CHICAGO PRESS
CHICAGO & LONDON

© 1967 by The University of Chicago

Published 1967   All rights reserved

Printed and bound by CPI Group (UK) Ltd, Croydon, CR0 4YY

ISBN-13: 978-0-226-06576-2 (paper)
ISBN-10: 0-226-06576-6 (paper)

PREFACE

The papers in this collection were all delivered at a five-day Liberal Arts Conference sponsored by the undergraduate College of the University of Chicago, as its contribution to the University's seventy-fifth anniversary celebration. When planning for the conference began, nobody knew, of course, precisely what a liberal arts conference might be, or whether a college could hold one worth holding. Everyone seemed to agree that the liberal arts were once again in a time of crisis, and that we might profit by trying once more to define those arts and to describe their possible relevance today. It was also quite clear that we should not attempt to produce consensus in a small, isolated group of conferees, but rather the kind of open debate among faculty and students that might justify the loss of nearly a week of class time.

The papers collected here report something of the lively controversy that resulted, but of course they cannot capture the chaotic exhilaration that kept most of our students on campus throughout a "free" mid-winter week when both Fort Lauderdale and the ski-slopes beckoned: the dinners in dormitories, faculty homes, and student apartments; the many seminars, panels, and unscheduled debates; the chance encounters when faculty and students, released from the pressure of classes, met on sidewalks, in halls, in cafeterias. There was no tape recorder present, for example, when Richard Lewontin, biologist, and Richard McKeon, philosopher, met in the Commons for a lengthy *ad hoc* debate on general education; nobody transcribed conversations like the one I had with one of our brightest science majors, who told me, in all solemnity,

---

* Of the many faculty members and students who helped with the conference, Mr. Robert Albrecht deserves special acknowledgment for his skill in co-ordinating what was, by its nature, wide-ranging and diffuse.

of the "two fundamental assumptions" which he had been forced to change during the week.

Such unprogrammed moments depended in part on the program of papers collected here. Whether or not the papers can now reproduce such effects, they do reflect the variety and the range (not to say the disorder and hybris) of the conference, just as the conference reflected the world's lack of clarity about higher education. Every paper deals in some way, directly or indirectly, with what undergraduate education should be; that question is, after all, implied by our modified version of Herbert Spencer's "What Knowledge is of Most Worth?" But beyond suggesting that we should continue to have undergraduate education that is not simply pre-professional, the authors show little agreement, either in definitions or in proposals.

Although many other themes and controversies could be traced through the volume, it is perhaps the implied confrontation about the proper meaning of "general education" that is most prominent. Particular "knowledges" are available in endless supply; universities and colleges are slowly suffocating under supplies of knowledge that did not threaten earlier generations. The search for a way of choosing, as implied by our topic, is an invitation to construct an education that is "general" in some sense.

Facing the problem systematically, Richard McKeon in his paper distinguishes four ways in which education can be general. Although we did not, unfortunately, have his distinctions before us until the third day, they can be useful in sorting through the contributions. In McKeon's view, general education can be the search for a common learning to be shared by *all men;* the search for principles or structures underlying *all knowledge;* the search for a learning appropriate to or useful for *all experience;* and the search for a learning derived from or applicable to *all cultures*. Each of these conceptions appears often in this volume, but their relative importance shifts from author to author.

The conception of a shared learning, suited to the needs of all men, dominates the papers by F. Champion Ward and myself. Like most of the participants, Ward is interested in all four kinds of general education; he has a good deal to say especially about what education can be translated from culture to culture. But he sees the main aim of the college, whether eastern or western, as "a common education in principles permitting communication and rational progress to occur among citizens otherwise variously expert and occupied." For him "the college program should have the same degree of coherence for its students and teachers as does a course of professional study." In this view it is natural that there should be a chronological division between the "general" and the "special" years, though Ward is willing to settle for new ways of turning special fields to realize liberal ends. In my own paper, similarly, I offer students one more defense, perhaps in the "panic-stricken tone" which Northrop Frye in his paper attributes to such defenses, of a liberal education that is essentially for all students, regardless of professional plans. In neither of these views do chronology and labels matter much; the indispensable "general" ability to read and write, for example, is developed better by some law schools than by most "general education" courses. But the shared pursuit of a common learning matters a great deal.

When attention is shifted to the second notion of "general," the search for principles or structures common to many (or all) fields, the usual distinction between general and special is likely to break down even further. Most of the papers here acknowledge as much, but Edward Levi makes the breakdown most explicit. Although he would not deny the need for some learning in common, he urges that the sharp division between general and specialized education be abandoned, in the name of improving specialized courses by making them more "generally" relevant: "the distinction between general education courses as liberal arts courses, on the one hand, and specialized courses as non-liberal but graduate on the other, has been stultifying to the college and to the divisions. It avoids the major aspect of one basic problem of undergraduate education today, the necessity to see and develop specialized courses so that they do indeed reflect the astonishing wonders of reality within a larger intellectual setting." With his attention similarly on the "special years," John Simpson asks for an innovation that would apply to perhaps as few as twenty of our most advanced students of the physical sciences. For him, genuine education in the sciences really begins when the students "are getting the feel for conducting research." But it is clear, although he doesn't put it this way, that he would think "the feel for research" a *general* value underlying all scientific inquiry.

With a similar concern for involving students with the essential operations of learning rather than with inert information, Richard McKeon pursues the new "encyclopedia," the *enkuklios paideia,* the circle of learning or "general education" that might be pursued in our time; it is a circle that is necessarily made up of essential methods and intellectual structures, not of the limitless subject matters and conclusions that offer themselves to us. Sir John Cockcroft, on the other hand, constructs an encyclopedia of knowledge that any educated man ought to have or desire, or that men in general would like to obtain; while his exhaustive listing might, in one interpretation, merely serve to underline the futility of attempting any sort of institutional plan for college education, it can also serve to dramatize our plight if we fail to choose.

While still pursuing the search for basic disciplines ("the

instruments of mental production") Northrop Frye and James Redfield both shift our attention to the third meaning of "general education." Here the goal of all education, "general" or "special," is a kind of character or wisdom that cannot easily be said to belong exclusively to any one stage or subject matter or discipline—or even to academic experience—but which is obviously the mark of a genuinely educated man. For Redfield the desired wisdom is found in the "knowledge of how to be free"; for Frye, in the freedom that comes with "the power to realize the possibilities of human life"; for both, this freedom depends on a Platonic vision of what Frye calls "the continuing city," Redfield "the knowledge that we cannot acquire but can only aspire to by living—and discoursing— together." The wisdom most worth having, in this view, is not likely to result from a fixed curriculum of "general education"; even if we could isolate the "creative arts" and embody them in courses, our ultimate goal—a quality of person—will remain elusive, unprogrammable, and finally beyond formulation. And on the other hand, even the narrowest of specialties can be taught in ways that will liberate to wisdom. As Frye says, "Every field of knowledge is the center of all knowledge, and general education should help the student to see how this is true for his chosen field." "The only knowledge that is worthwhile is the knowledge that leads to wisdom, for knowledge without wisdom is a body without life. But no form of knowledge necessarily does or cannot do that: the completing of the structure has something to do with one's sense of the place of knowledge in the total human situation, ideal as well as actual."

With all this variety of emphasis, I think it could be argued that everyone here returns finally, if only by implication, to the first notion, a learning desirable for all men. Ann Scott, for example, might seem at first to be defending a specialized education for women. But it is quite clear that her plea for special courses for women is really defended in the name of goals that are common to men and women. What "all men" should know should be known by women in a special way—as a woman will want to know not just what it means to be human and to act freely as a human being but what it means to be a woman and to act freely as a woman. Thus the reading list for women may look different, but the goals are the goals of liberal education. Even her insistence on the provision of a field of specialization is stated as a way of fulfilling what clearly are for her desirable educational goals for all men and women: a sense of mastery, of competence, of self-respect.

In a similar way, John Platt's call for diversity, which might sound at first like a cry against a common learning, could easily be interpreted as a plea to discover what kind of education will produce, in all men, the greatest inventiveness, the greatest willingness to undertake intellectual adventure, the greatest capacity to combat the commonplace and repetitive. In this view, the knowledge most worth having for everyone will be the knowledge of how to be creatively different from everyone else, specialized in one's own unique direction; but this knowledge, allowing for maximum diversity, will be the same kind of knowledge needed by all. The paradox of education for freedom or diversity is that, in the end, thought is not foot-loose or truth uncontrollably diverse. Mastery of the instruments of mental production will require, finally, that all men traverse some common educational ground. If a love of diversity is a valuable goal, it is good for all and hence not really diverse; if we take it seriously it will lead us to a common learning—regardless of differences in reading lists or methods that may appear on the surface.

By such half-playful crosscuttings and redefinitions does an editor find common ground in diverse talk about freedom and diversity. The trick is relatively easy, working with minds as like-minded as these, but even so, it is not easy to say what curriculum these men and women would agree to offer. Whether from the baffling confusion reigning in higher education today we can extract forms of learning demonstrably more worthy of pursuit than others is not a settled question, even if I am right in thinking that we all engage in silent ranking. But it is hard to see how the American college can survive as an institution functionally distinct from graduate and professional schools unless in some sense we can agree on a knowledge most worth having.

CONTENTS

CONTENTS

IS THERE ANY KNOWLEDGE
THAT A MAN *MUST* HAVE?

Wayne C. Booth

As you have no doubt already recognized, my topic is simply a more exasperating form of the general topic of this conference. All of the ambiguities and annoyances that are stirred up when we ask what is most worth knowing are brought to the boiling point when we ask whether some things really *must* be known.

Such questions are not faced cheerfully by most of us in this empirical generation. It is true, of course, that we regularly make choices that are based on implied standards of what is worth knowing. We set degree requirements, we organize courses, we give examinations, and we would scarcely want to say that what we do is entirely arbitrary. We conduct research on this rather than that subject, and we urge our students in this rather than that direction; though we may profess a happy relativism of goals, as if all knowledge were equally valuable, we cannot and do not run our lives or our universities on entirely relativistic assumptions. And yet we seem to be radically unwilling to discuss the ground for our choices; it is almost as if we expected that a close look would reveal a scandal at the heart of our academic endeavor. The journals are full, true enough, of breast-beating and soul-searching, especially since "Berkeley." But you will look a long while before you find any discussion of what is worth knowing. You will look even longer before you find anything written in the past ten years worthy of being

At the conference, a much shortened version of this talk was delivered.

entered into the great debate on liberal education,[1] as it is represented by the selections in the "syllabus" prepared for this conference.[2] When Herbert Spencer, for example, wrote the essay from which we paraphrased our title, he knew that he addressed a public steeped in a tradition of careful argument about "What Knowledge Is of Most Worth." Though he disagreed with the traditional practice of placing classical studies at the center of liberal education, he knew that he could not defend scientific education simply by asserting its superiority. The very tradition he was attacking had educated an audience that required him to argue his case as cogently as possible, and, at the same time, it gave him confidence that his readers would think his question both important and amenable to productive discussion.

We were able to feel no such confidence in calling for a similar debate within a major university in 1966. Even at the University of Chicago, which has been more hospitable than most universities to serious controversy about the aims of education, we expected that the threat of hierarchical judgment implied by our topic would make men nervous. And we were right. "You will simply stir up meaningless controversy," one faculty member complained. "Since nobody can say what is most worth knowing, you'll get as many opinions as there are people, and the debate will be pointless." One bright fourth-year student said, "In choosing my major I've already chosen the knowledge which *for me* is most worth having. Each man chooses his own answers to this question, and the right choice for you is not the right choice for me."

[1] Since the conference, one fine exception has appeared, Daniel Bell's *The Reforming of General Education* (New York: Columbia University Press, 1966).

[2] The "syllabus" contained works like the following: "Liberal Knowledge Its Own End" by Cardinal Newman; "What Knowledge Is of Most Worth" by Herbert Spencer; selections from *The Education of Henry Adams;* "Science As a Vocation" by Max Weber; and *The Great Conversation* by Robert M. Hutchins.

And then—curiously enough—he repeated what I had heard earlier from the faculty member: "You'll get as many answers as there are men discussing."

Well, first of all, even if we think of knowledge as inert information, something that we can *have,* this simply is not so. There are not enough opinions about what is worth knowing to provide each of us with a custom-built model of his own. In the past few months, I have heard hundreds of defenses of this or that body of information or pattern of skills as worth learning, but there have been nothing like hundreds of different views. I suspect that a bit of logical sorting would reveal no more than twenty or thirty distinct views in this community, and perhaps no more than a good round dozen.

I raise what may seem like little more than a quibble because I think it is important at the beginning of this conference to recognize what our topic asks of us. Taken seriously, it not only asks us to affirm what we think is educationally important; we're all ready enough to do that at the drop of a hat. What is troublesome is that it asks us to reason together about our various preferences, and it assumes that some answers to the question will be better than others—not just preferable to you or to me, because of the way we have been educated, but better, period (or as men used to say, better, absolutely). It does not, of course, assume that finding answers will be easy; we cannot, like some non-academics, discover an indictment of the "knowledge factories" simply by ferreting out thesis topics that sound ridiculous. But it does assume that there is something irrational in our contemporary neglect of systematic thought about educational goals. Scholars in the middle ages are often accused of having automatically assumed hierarchies in every subject. Many of us as automatically assume that value judgments among types or bits of knowledge are irrelevant. Yet we cannot escape implying, by our practice, that though all "knowledges" are equal, some are more equal than others. Our choice of topic asks us to attempt, during this conference, to think seriously about the ground for the hierarchies that our practical choices imply.

2

Everyone lives on the assumption that a great deal of knowledge is not worth bothering about; though we all know that what looks trivial in one man's hands may turn out to be earth-shaking in another's, we simply cannot know very much, compared with what might be known, and we must therefore choose. What is shocking is not the act of choice which we all commit openly but the claim that some choices are wrong. Especially shocking is the claim implied by my title: There is some knowledge that a man *must* have.

There clearly is no such thing, if by knowledge we mean mere acquaintance with this or that thing, fact, concept, literary work, or scientific law. When C. P. Snow and F. R. Leavis exchanged blows on whether knowledge of Shakespeare is more important than knowledge of the second law of thermodynamics, they were both, it seemed to me, much too ready to assume as indispensable what a great many wise and good men have quite obviously got along without. And it is not only non-professionals who can survive in happy ignorance of this or that bit of lore. I suspect that many successful scientists (in biology, say) have lost whatever hold they might once have had on the second law; I know that a great many literary scholars survive and even flourish without knowing certain "indispensable" classics. We all get along without vast loads of learning that other men take as necessary marks of an educated man. If we once begin to "reason the need" we will find, like Lear, that "our basest beggars/Are in the poorest thing superfluous." Indeed, we can survive, in a manner of speaking, even in the modern world, with little more than the bare literacy necessary to tell the "off" buttons from the "on."

Herbert Spencer would remind us at this point that we are interpreting *need* as if it were entirely a question of private survival. Though he talks about what a man must know to stay alive, he is more interested, in his defense of science, in what a *society* must know to survive: "Is there any knowledge that *man* must have?"—not *a* man, but *man*. This question is put to us much more acutely in our time than it was in Spencer's, and it is by no means as easy to argue now as it was then that the knowledge needed for man's survival is scientific knowledge. The threats of atomic annihilation, of engulfing population growth, of depleted air, water, and food must obviously be met, if man is to survive, and in meeting them man will, it is true, need more and more scientific knowledge; but it is not at all clear that more and more scientific knowledge will by itself suffice. Even so, a modern Herbert Spencer might well argue that a conference like this one, with its emphasis on the individual and his cognitive needs, is simply repeating the mistakes of the classical tradition. The knowledge most worth having would be, from his point of view, that of how to pull mankind through the next century or so without absolute self-destruction. The precise proportions of different kinds of knowledge—physical, biological, political, ethical, psychological, historical, or whatever—would be different from those prescribed in Spencer's essay, but the nature of the search would be precisely the same.

We can admit the relevance of this emphasis on social utility and at the same time argue that our business here is with other matters entirely. If the only knowledge a man *must* have is how to cross the street without getting knocked down—or, in other words, how to navigate the centuries without blowing himself up—then we may as well close the conference and go home. We may as well also roll up the college and mail it to a research institute, because almost any place that is not cluttered up with notions of liberal education will be able to discover and transmit practical bits of survival-lore better than we can. Our problem of survival is a rather different one, thrust at us as soon as we change our title slightly once again to "Is there any knowledge (other than the knowledge for survival) that *a* man must have?" That slight shift opens a new perspective on the problem, because the question of what it is to be a man, of what it is to be fully human, is the question at the heart of liberal education.

To be human, to be human, to be fully human. What does it mean? What is required? Immediately, we start feeling nervous again. Is the speaker suggesting that some of us are not fully human *yet?* Here come those hierarchies again. Surely in our pluralistic society we can admit an unlimited number of legitimate ways to be a man, without prescribing some outmoded aristocratic code!

3

Who—or what—is the creature we would educate? Our answer will determine our answers to educational questions, and it is therefore, I think, worth far more vigorous effort than it usually receives. I find it convenient, and only slightly unfair, to classify the educational talk I encounter these days under four notions of man, three of them metaphorical, only one literal. Though nobody's position, I suppose, fits my types neatly, some educators talk as if they were programming machines, some talk as if they were conditioning rats, some talk as if they were training ants to take a position in the anthill, and some—precious few—talk as if they thought of themselves as men dealing with men.

One traditional division of the human soul, you will remember, was into three parts: the vegetable, the animal, and the rational. Nobody, so far as I know, has devised an educational program treating students as vegetables, though one runs into the analogy used negatively in academic sermons from time to time. Similarly, no one ever really says that men are ants, though there is a marvelous passage in Kwame Nkrumah's autobiography in which he meditates longingly on the order and pure functionality of an anthill. Educators do talk of men as machines or as animals, but of course they always point out that men are much more complicated than any other known animals or machines. My point here is not so much to attack any one of these metaphors—dangerous as I think they are—but to describe briefly what answers to our question each of them might suggest.

Ever since Descartes, La Mettrie, and others explicitly called man a machine, the metaphor has been a dominant one in educational thinking. Some have thought of man as a very complex machine, needing very elaborate programming; others have thought of him as a very simple machine, requiring little more than a systematic pattern of stimuli to produce foretellable responses. I heard a psychologist recently repeat the old behaviorist claim (first made by John B. Watson, I believe) that if you would give him complete control over any normal child's life from birth, he could turn that child into a great musician or a great mathematician or a great poet—you name it and he could produce it. On being pressed, the professor admitted that this claim was only "in theory," because we don't yet have the necessary knowledge. When I pushed further by asking why he was so confident in advance of experimental proof, it became clear that his faith in the fundamental metaphor of man as a programmable machine was unshakable.

When the notion of man as machine was first advanced, the machine was a very simple collection of pulleys and billiard balls and levers. Such original simplicities have been badly battered by our growing awareness both of how complex real machines can be and of how much more complex man is than any known machine. Modern notions of stimulus-response patterns are immeasurably more complicated than anything Descartes imagined, because we are now aware of the fantastic variety of stimuli that the man-machine is subject to and of the even more fantastic complexity of the responding circuits.

But whether the machine is simple or complex, the educational task for those who think of man under this metaphor is to program the mechanism so that it will produce the results that we have foreordained. We do not simply fill the little pitchers, like Mr. Gradgrind in Dickens' *Hard Times;* we are much too sophisticated to want only undigested "pour-back," as he might have called his product. But we still program the information channels so that the proper if-loops and do-loops will be followed and the right feedback produced. The "programming" can be done by human teachers, of course, and not only by machines; but it is not surprising that those whose thinking is dominated by this metaphor tend to discover that machines are better teachers than men. The more ambitious programmers do not hesitate to claim that they can teach both thought and creativity in this way. But I have yet to see a program that can deal effectively with any subject that cannot be reduced to simple yes and no answers, that is, to answers that are known in advance by the programmer and can thus be fixed for all time.

We can assume that subtler machines will be invented that can engage in simulated dialogue with the pupil, and perhaps even recognize when a particularly bright pupil has discovered something new that refutes the program. But even the subtlest teaching machine imaginable will still be subject, one must assume, to a final limitation: it can teach only what a machine can "learn." For those who believe that man is literally nothing but a very complicated machine, this is not in fact a limitation; machines will ultimately be able to duplicate all mental processes, thus "learning" everything learnable, and they will be able in consequence to teach everything.

I doubt this claim for many reasons, and I am glad to find the testimony of Norbert Wiener, the first and best known cyberneticist, to the effect that there will always remain a radical gap between computers and the human mind. But "ultimately" is a long way off, and I am not so much concerned with whether ultimately man's mind will closely resemble some ultimately inventable machine as I am with the effects, here and now, of thinking about men under the analogy with machines of today. Let me simply close this section with an illustration of how the mechanistic model can permeate our thought in destructive ways. Ask yourselves what picture of creature-to-be-educated emerges from this professor of teacher education:

> To implement the TEAM Project new curriculum proposal . . . our first concerns are with instructional systems, materials to feed the system, and personnel to operate the system. We have defined an instructional system as the optimal blending of the demands of content, communication, and learning. While numerous models

have been developed, our simplified model of an instructional system would look like Figure 2. . . . We look at the process of communication—communicating content to produce learning—as something involving the senses: . . . [aural, oral, tactile, visual]. And I think in teacher education we had better think of the communications aspect of the instructional system as a package that includes the teacher, textbook, new media, classroom, and environment. To integrate these elements to more effectively transmit content into permanent learning, new and better instructional materials are needed and a new focus on the teacher of teachers is required. The teacher of teachers must: (1) examine critically the content of traditional courses in relation to desired behavioral outcomes; (2) become more sophisticated in the techniques of communicating course content; and (3) learn to work in concert with media specialists to develop the materials and procedures requisite to the efficient instructional system. And if the media specialist were to be charged with the efficient operation of the system, his upgrading would demand a broad-based "media generalist" orientation.[3]

I submit that the author of this passage was thinking of human beings as stimulus-response systems on the simplest possible model, and that he was thinking of the purpose of education as the transfer of information from one machine to another. Though he would certainly deny it if we asked him, he has come to think about the human mind so habitually in the mechanistic mode that he doesn't even know he's doing it.[4]

But it is time to move from the machine metaphor to animal metaphors. They are closely related, of course, because every-

---

[3] Desmond P. Wedberg, *Teacher Education Looks to the Future*, Twelfth Biennial School for Executives (Washington, D. C.: American Association of Colleges for Teacher Education, 1964).

[4] I am not of course suggesting that *any* use of teaching machines implies a mechanistic reduction of persons to machines; programmers rightly point out that machines *can* free teachers from the mechanical and save time for the personal.

body who believes that man is a machine also believes that animals are machines, only simpler ones. But many people who would resist the word "machine" do tend to analogize man to one or another characteristic of animals. Since man is obviously an animal in one sense, he can be studied as an animal, and he can be taught as an animal is taught. Most of the fundamental research in learning theory underlying the use of teaching machines has been done, in fact, on animals like rats and pigeons. You can teach pigeons to play Ping-Pong rather quickly by rewarding every gesture they make that moves them toward success in the game and refusing to reward those gestures that you want to efface. Though everybody admits that human beings are more complicated than rats and pigeons, just as everyone admits that human beings are more complicated than computers, the basic picture of the animal as a collection of drives or instincts, "conditioned" to learn according to rewards or punishments, has underlain much modern educational theory.

The notion of the human being as a collection of drives different from animal drives only in being more complex carries with it implications for educational planners. If you and I are motivated only by sex or hunger or more complex drives like desire for power or for ego-satisfaction, then of course all education depends on the provision of satisfactions along our route to knowledge. If our teachers can just program carrots along the path at the proper distance, we donkey-headed students will plod along the path from carrot to carrot and end up as educated men.

I cannot take time here to deal with this view adequately, but it seems to me that it is highly questionable even about animals themselves. What kind of thing, really, is a rat or a monkey? The question of whether animals have souls has been debated actively for at least nine centuries; now psychologists find themselves dealing with the same question under another guise: What *are* these little creatures that we kill so blithely for the sake of knowledge? What *are* these strangely resistant little bundles of energy that will prefer —as experiments with rats have shown—a complicated interesting maze without food to a dull one *with* food?

There are, in fact, many experiments by now showing that at the very least we must postulate, for animals, a strong independent drive for mastery of the environment or satisfaction of curiosity about it. All the more advanced animals will learn to push levers that produce interesting results— clicks or bells or flashing lights or sliding panels—when no other reward is offered.[5] It seems clear that even to be a fulfilled animal, as it were, something more than "animal satisfaction" is needed!

I am reminded here of the experiments on mother-love in monkeys reported by Harry F. Harlow in the *Scientific American* some years ago. Harlow called his article "Love in Infant Monkeys," and the subtitle of his article read, "Affection in infants was long thought to be generated by the satisfactions of feeding. Studies of young rhesus monkeys now indicate that love derives mainly from close bodily contact." The experiment consisted of giving infant monkeys a choice between a plain wire figure that offered the infant milk and a terry-cloth covered figure without milk. There was a pathetic picture of an infant clinging to the terry-cloth figure, and a caption that read "The infants spent most of their time clinging to the soft cloth 'mother' even when nursing bottles were attached to the wire mother." The article concluded— rather prematurely, I thought—that "contact comfort" had

[5] See Robert W. White, "Motivation Reconsidered: The Concept of Competence," *Psychological Review*, 66 (1959), 297–333.

been shown to be a "prime requisite in the formation of an infant's love for its mother," that the act of nursing had been shown to be unimportant if not totally irrelevant in forming such love (though it was evident to any reader, even at the time, that no genuine "*act* of nursing" had figured in the experiment at all), and that "our investigations have established a secure experimental approach to this realm of dramatic and subtle emotional relationships." The only real problem, Harlow said, was the availability of enough infant monkeys for experiment.

Now I would not want to underrate the importance of Harlow's demonstration to the scientific community that monkeys do not live by bread alone. But I think that most scientists and humanists reading that article would have been struck by two things. The first is the automatic assumption that the way to study a subject like love is to break it down into its component parts; nobody looking at that little monkey clinging to the terry-cloth could possibly have said, "This is love," unless he had been blinded by a hidden conviction that love in animals is—must be—a mere cumulative result of a collection of drive satisfactions. This assumption is given quite plainly in Harlow's concluding sentence: "Finally with such techniques established, there appears to be no reason why we cannot at some future time investigate the fundamental neurophysiological and biochemical variables underlying affection and love." For Harlow monkeys (and people) seem to be mere collections of neurophysiological and biochemical variables, and love will be best explained when we can explain the genesis of each of its parts. The second striking point is that for Harlow animals do not matter, except as they are useful for experiment. If he had felt that they mattered, he might have noticed the look on his infant's face—a look that predicted for me, and for other readers of the *Scientific American* I've talked with, that these monkeys were doomed.

And indeed they were. A year or so later another article appeared, reporting Harlow's astonished discovery that all of the little monkeys on which he had earlier experimented had turned out to be incurably psychotic. Not a single monkey could mate, not a single monkey could play, not a single monkey could in fact become anything more than the twisted half-creatures that Harlow's deprivations had made of them. Harlow's new discovery was that monkeys needed close association with their peers during infancy and that such association was even more important to their development than genuine mothering. There was no sign that Harlow had learned any fundamental lessons from his earlier gross mistakes; he had landed nicely on his feet, still convinced that the way to study love is to break it down into its component parts and that the way to study animals is to maim them or reduce them to something less than themselves. As Robert White says, summarizing his reasons for rejecting similar methods in studying human infancy, it is too often assumed that the scientific way is to analyze behavior until one can find a small enough unit to allow for detailed research, but in the process "very vital common properties" are lost from view.

I cite Harlow's two reports not, of course, to attack animal experimentation—though I must confess that I am horrified by much that goes on in its name—nor to claim that animals are more like human beings than they are. Rather, I want simply to suggest that the danger of thinking of men as animals is heightened if the animals we think of are reduced to machines on a simple model.

The effects of reducing education to conditioning can be

seen throughout America today. Usually they appear in subtle forms, disguised with the language of personalism; you will look a long time before you find anyone (except a very few Skinnerians) saying that he thinks of education as exactly like conditioning pigeons. But there are plenty of honest, blunt folk around to let the cat out of the bag—like the author of an article this year in *College Composition and Communication:* "The Use of a Multiple Response Device in the Teaching of Remedial English." The author claimed to have evidence that if you give each student four buttons to be pushed on multiple-choice questions, with all the buttons wired into a lighted grid at the front of the room, the resulting "instantaneous feedback"—every child learning immediately whether he agrees with the rest of the class— speeds up the learning of grammatical rules considerably over the usual workbook procedures. I daresay it does—but meanwhile what has happened to education? Or take the author of an article on "Procedures and Techniques of Teaching," who wrote as follows: "If we expect students to learn skills, they have to practice, but practice doesn't make perfect. Practice works if the learner *learns the results* of his practice, i.e., if he receives feedback. Feedback is most effective when it is contiguous to the response being learned. One of the chief advantages of teaching machines is that the learner finds out quickly whether his response is right or wrong . . . [Pressey] has published the results of an extensive program of research with tests that students score for themselves by punching alternatives until they hit the correct one. . . . [Thus] teaching machines or workbooks have many theoretical advantages over lecturing or other conventional methods of instruction." But according to what theory, one must ask, *do* systematic feedback mechanisms, perfected to whatever degree, have "theoretical advantages" over human contact? Whatever else can be said for such a theory, it will be based on the simplest of comparisons with animal learning. Unfortunately, the author goes on, experimental evidence is on the whole rather discouraging: "Experiments at the Systems Development Corporation . . . suggest that teaching incorporating . . . human characteristics is more effective than the typical fixed-sequence machines. (In this experiment instead of using teaching machines to simulate human teachers, the experimenters used humans to simulate teaching machines!)"

So far I have dealt with analogies for man that apply only to individuals. My third analogy turns to the picture of men in groups, and it is given to me partly by discussions of education, like those of Admiral Rickover, that see it simply as filling society's needs. I know of only one prominent educator who has publicly praised the anthill as a model for the kind of society a university should serve—a society of specialists each trained to do his part. But the notion pervades many of the defenses of the emerging multiversities.

If knowledge is needed to enable men to function as units in society, and if the health of society is taken as the purpose of their existence, then there is nothing wrong in training the ants to fill their niches; it would be wrong not to. "Education is our first line of defense—make it strong," so reads the title of the first chapter of Admiral Rickover's book, *Education and Freedom* (New York: Dutton, 1959). "We must upgrade our schools" in order to "guarantee the future prosperity and freedom of the Republic." You can tell whether the ant-analogy is dominating a man's thinking by a simple test of how he orders his ends and means. In Admiral Rickover's statement, the schools must be upgraded in order to guarantee future prosperity, that is, we improve education for the sake of some presumed social good.

I seldom find anyone putting it the other way round: we must guarantee prosperity so that we can improve the schools, and the reason we want to improve the schools is that we want to insure the development of certain kinds of persons, both as teachers and as students. You cannot even say what I just said so long as you are really thinking of ants and anthills. Ants are not ends in themselves, ultimately more valuable than the hills they live in (I *think* they are not; maybe to themselves, or in the eyes of God, even ants are ultimate, self-justifying ends). At least from our point of view, ants are expendable, or to put it another way, their society is more beautiful, more interesting, more admirable than they are. And I would want to argue that too many people think of human beings in the same way when they think of educating them. The Communists make this quite explicit: the ends of Communist society justify whatever distortion or destruction of individual purposes is necessary to achieve them; men are educated for the state, not for their own well-being. They are basically political animals, not in the Aristotelian sense that they require society if they are to achieve their full natures and thus their own special, human kind of happiness, but in the sense that they exist, like ants, for the sake of the body politic.

If the social order is the final justification of what we do in education, then a certain attitude toward teaching and research will result: all of us little workmen, down inside the anthill, will go on happily contributing our tiny bit to the total scheme without worrying much about larger questions of the why and wherefore. I know a graduate student who says that she sometimes sees her graduate professors as an army of tiny industrious miners at the bottom of a vast mine, chipping away at the edges and shipping their bits of knowledge up to the surface, blindly hoping that someone up there will know what to do with it all. An order is received for such-and-such new organic compounds; society needs them. Another order is received for an atomic bomb; it is needed, and it is therefore produced. Often no orders come down, but the chipping goes on anyway, and the shipments are made, because everyone knows that the health of the mine depends on a certain tonnage of specialized knowledge each working day.

We have learned lately that "they" are going to establish a great new atom-smasher, perhaps near Chicago. The atom-smasher will employ two thousand scientists and technicians. I look out at you here, knowing that some of you are physics majors, and I wonder whether any of you will ultimately be employed in that new installation, and if you are, whether it will be as an ant or as a human being. Which it will be must depend not on your ultimate employers but on yourself and on what happens to your education between now and then: if you have been given nothing but training to be that ultimate unit in that ultimate system, only a miracle can save you from formic dissolution of your human lineaments.

4

But it is long past time for me to turn from these negative, truncated portraits of what man really is not and attempt to say what he is. And here we encounter a difficulty that I find very curious. You will note that each of these metaphors has reduced man to something less than man, or at least to a partial aspect of man. It is easy to say that man is not a machine, though he is in some limited respects organized like a machine and even to some degree "programmable." It is also easy to say that man is not simply a complicated rat or monkey, though he is in some ways like rats and monkeys. Nor is man an ant, though he lives and must function in a complicated social milieu. All these metaphors break down not because they are flatly false but because they *are* metaphors, and any metaphorical definition is inevitably misleading. The ones I have been dealing with are especially misleading, because in every case they have reduced something more complex to something much less complex. But even if we were to analogize man to something more complex, say, the universe, we would be dissatisfied. What we want is some notion of what man really *is,* so that we will know what or whom we are trying to educate.

And here it is that we discover something very important about man, something that even the least religious person must find himself mystified by: man is the one "thing" we know that is completely resistant to our efforts at metaphor or analogy or image-making. What seems to be the most important literal characteristic of man is his resistance to definitions in terms of anything else. If you call me a machine, even a very complicated machine, I know that you deny what I care most about, my selfhood, my sense of being a person, my consciousness, my conviction of freedom and dignity, my awareness of love, my laughter. Machines have none of these things, and even if we were generous to their prospects, and imagined machines immeasurably superior to the most complicated ones now in existence, we would still feel an infinite gap between them and what we know to be a basic truth about ourselves: machines are expendable, ultimately expendable, and men are mysteriously ends in themselves.

I hear people deny this, but when they do they always argue for their position by claiming marvelous feats of super-machine calculation that machines can now do or will someday be able to do. But that is not the point; of course machines can outcalculate us. The question to ask is entirely a different one: Will they ever outlove us, outlive us, out-value us? Do we build machines because machines are good things in themselves? Do we nurture them for their own good, as we nurture our children? An obvious way to test our sense of worth in men and machines is to ask ourselves whether we would ever campaign to liberate the poor drowntrodden machines who have been enslaved. Shall we form a National Association for the Advancement of Machinery? Will anyone ever feel a smidgeon of moral indignation because this or that piece of machinery is not given equal rights before the law? Or put it another way: Does anyone value Gemini more than the twins? There may be men now alive who would rather "destruct," as we say, the pilot than the experimental rocket, but most of us still believe that the human being in the space ship is more important than the space ship.

When college students protest the so-called depersonalization of education, what they mean, finally, is not simply that they want to meet their professors socially or that they want small classes or that they do not want to be dealt with by IBM machines. All these things are but symptoms of a deeper sense of a violation of their literal reality as persons, ends in themselves rather than mere expendable things. Similarly, the current deep-spirited revolt against racial and economic injustice seems to me best explained as a sudden assertion that people, of whatever color or class, are not reducible to social conveniences. When you organize your labor force or your educational system as if men were mere social conveniences, "human resources," as we say, contributors to the gross national product, you violate something that we all know, in a form of knowledge much deeper than our knowledge of the times tables or the second law of thermodynamics: those field hands, those children crowded into the deadening classroom, those men laboring without dignity in the city ant-hills are *men*, creatures whose worth is mysteriously more than any description of it we might make in justifying what we do to them.

5

Ants, rats, and machines can all learn a great deal. Taken together, they "know" a very great part of what our schools and colleges are now designed to teach. But is there any kind of knowledge that a creature must have to qualify as a man? Is there any part of the educational task that is demanded of us by virtue of our claim to educate this curious entity, this *person* that cannot be reduced to mechanism or animality alone?

You will not be surprised, by now, to have me sound, in my answer, terribly traditional, not to say square: the education that a *man* must have is what has traditionally been called liberal education. The knowledge it yields is the knowledge or capacity or power of how to act freely as a man. That's why we call liberal education liberal: it is intended to liberate from whatever it is that makes animals act like animals and machines act like machines.

I'll return in a moment to what it means to act freely as a man. But we are already in a position to say something about what knowledge a man must have—he must first of all be able to learn for himself. If he cannot learn for himself, he is enslaved by his teachers' ideas, or by the ideas of his more persuasive contemporaries, or by machines programmed by other men. He may have what we call a good formal education, yet still be totally bound by whatever opinions happen to have come his way in attractive garb. One wonders how many of our graduates have learned how to take hold of a subject and "work it up," so that they can make themselves experts on what other men have concluded. In some ways this is not a very demanding goal, and it is certainly not very exciting. It says nothing about that popular concept, creativity, or about imagination or originality. All it says is that anyone who is dependent on his teachers *is* dependent, not free, and that anyone who knows how to learn for himself is less like animals and machines than anyone who does not know how to learn for himself.

We see already that a college is not being merely capricious or arbitrary when it insists that some kinds of learning are more important than some others. The world is overflowing with interesting subjects and valuable skills, but surely any college worth the name will put first things first: it will try to insure, as one inescapable goal, that every graduate can dig out from the printed page what he needs to know. And it will not let the desire to tamp in additional tidbits of knowledge, however delicious, interfere with training minds for whom a formal teacher is no longer required.

To put our first goal in this way raises some real problems —perhaps even problems that we cannot solve. Obviously no college can produce self-learners in very many subjects. Are we not lucky if a graduate can learn for himself even in one field, now that knowledge in all areas has advanced as far as it has? Surely we cannot expect our graduates to reach a stage of independence in mathematics and physics, in political science and psychology, in philosophy and English, *and* in all the other nice subjects that one would like to master.

Rather than answer this objection right away, let me make things even more difficult by saying that it is not enough to learn how to learn. The man who cannot *think* for himself, going beyond what other men have learned or thought, is still enslaved to other men's ideas. Obviously the goal of learning to think is even more difficult than the goal of learning to learn. But difficult as it is we must add it to our list. It is simply not enough to be able to get up a subject on one's own, like a good encyclopaedia employee, even though any college would take pride if all its graduates could do so. To be fully human means in part to think one's own thoughts, to reach a point at which, whether one's ideas are different from or similar to other men's, they are truly one's own.

The art of asking oneself critical questions that lead either to new answers or to genuine revitalizing of old answers, the art of making thought live anew in each new generation, may not be entirely amenable to instruction. But it is a necessary art nonetheless, for any man who wants to be free. It is an art that all philosophers have tried to pursue, and many of them have given direct guidance in how to pursue it. Needless to say, it is an art the pursuit of which is never fully completed. No one thinks for himself very much of the time or in very many subjects. Yet the habitual effort to ask the right critical questions and to apply rigorous tests to our hunches is a clearer mark than any other of an educated man.

But again we stumble upon the question, "Learn to think about *what?*" The modern world presents us with innumerable subjects to think about. Does it matter whether anyone achieves this rare and difficult point in more than one subject? And if not, won't the best education simply be the one that brings a man into mastery of a narrow specialty as soon as possible, so that he can learn to think for himself as soon as possible? Even at best most of us are enslaved to opinions provided for us by experts in *most* fields. So far, it might be argued, I still have not shown that there is any kind of knowledge that a man must have, only that there are certain skills that he must be able to exercise in at least one field.

To provide a proper grounding for my answer to that objection would require far more time than I have left, and I'm not at all sure that I could do so even with all the time in the world. The question of whether it is possible to maintain a human stance toward any more than a tiny fraction of modern knowledge is not clearly answerable at this stage in our history. It will be answered, if at all, only when men have learned how to store and retrieve all "machinable" knowledge, freeing themselves for distinctively human tasks. But in the meantime, I find myself unable to surrender, as it were, three distinct kinds of knowledge that seem to me indispensable to being human.

To be a man, a man must first know something about his own nature and his place in Nature, with a capital N—something about the truth of things, as men used to say in the old-fashioned days before the word "truth" was banned from academia. Machines are not curious, so far as I can judge; animals are, but presumably they never go, in their philosophies, even at the furthest, beyond a kind of solipsistic existentialism. But in science, in philosophy (ancient and modern), in theology, in psychology and anthropology, and in literature (of some kinds), we are presented with accounts of our universe and of our place in it that as men we can respond to in only one manly way: by thinking about them, by speculating and testing our speculations.

We know before we start that our thought is doomed to incompleteness and error and downright chanciness. Even the most rigorously scientific view will be changed, we know, within a decade, or perhaps even by tomorrow. But to refuse the effort to understand is to resign from the human race; the unexamined life can no doubt be worth living in other respects—after all, it is no mean thing to be a vegetable, an oak tree, an elephant or a lion. But a man, a man will want to see, in this speculative domain, beyond his next dinner.

By putting it in this way, I think we can avoid the claim that to be a man I must have studied any one field—philosophy, science, theology, But to be a man, *I must speculate,* and I must learn how to test my speculations so that they are not simply capricious, unchecked by other men's speculations. A college education, surely, should throw every student into a regular torrent of speculation, and it should school him to recognize the different standards of validation proper to different kinds of claims to truth. You cannot distinguish a man who in this respect is educated from other men by whether or not he believes in God, or in UFOs. But you can tell an educated man by the way he takes hold of the question of whether God exists, or whether UFOs are from Mars. Do you know your own reasons for your beliefs, or do you absorb your beliefs from whatever happens to be in your environment, like plankton taking in nourishment?

Second, the man who has not learned how to make the great human achievements in the arts his own, who does not know what it means to *earn* a great novel or symphony or painting for himself, is enslaved either to caprice or to other men's testimony or to a life of ugliness. You will notice that as I turn thus to "beauty"—another old-fashioned term—I do not say that a man must know how to prove what is beautiful or how to discourse on aesthetics. Such speculative activities are pleasant and worthwhile in themselves, but they belong in my first domain. Here we are asking that a man be educated to the experience of beauty; speculation about it can then follow. My point is simply that a man is less than a man if he cannot respond to the art made by his fellow man.

Again I have tried to put the standard in a way that allows for the impossibility of any one man's achieving independent responses in very many arts. Some would argue that education should insure some minimal human competence in all of the arts, or at least in music, painting, and literature. I suppose I would be satisfied if all of our graduates had been "hooked" by at least one art, hooked so deeply that they could never get free. As in the domain of speculation, we could say that the more types of distinctively human activity a man can master, the better, but we are today talking about floors, not ceilings, and I shall simply rest content with saying that to be a man, a man must know artistic beauty, in some form, and know it in the way that beauty can be known. (The distinction between natural and man-made beauty might give me trouble if you pushed me on it here, but let me just say, dogmatically, that I would not be satisfied simply to know natural beauty—women and sunsets, say—as a substitute for art).

Finally, the man who has not learned anything about how to understand his own intentions and to make them effective in the world, who has not, through experience and books, learned something about what is possible and what impossible, what desirable and what undesirable, will be enslaved by the political and social intentions of other men, benign or malign. The domain of practical wisdom is at least as complex and troublesome as the other two, and at the same time it is even more self-evidently indispensable. How should a man live? How should a society be run? What direction should a university take in 1966? For that matter what should be the proportion, in a good university, of inquiry into truth, beauty, and "goodness"? What kind of knowledge of self or of society is pertinent to living the life proper to a man? In short, the very question of this conference falls within this final domain: What knowledge, if any, is most worthy of pursuit? You cannot distinguish the men from the boys according to any one set of conclusions, but you *can* recognize a man, in this domain, simply by discovering whether he can think for himself about practical questions, with some degree of freedom from blind psychological or political or economic compulsions. Ernest Hemingway tells somewhere of a man who had "moved one dollar's width to the [political] right for every dollar that he'd ever earned." Perhaps no man ever achieves the opposite extreme, complete freedom in his choices from irrelevant compulsions. But all of us who believe in education believe that it is possible for any man, through study and conscientious thought, to school his choices—that is, to free them through coming to understand the forces working on them.

6

Even from this brief discussion of the three domains, I think we are put in a position to see how it can be said that there is some knowledge that a man must have. The line I have been pursuing will not lead to a list of great books, or even to a list of indispensable departments in a university. Nor will it lead, in any clear-cut fashion, to a pattern of requirements in each of the divisions. Truth, beauty, and goodness (or "right choice") are relevant to study in every division within the university; the humanities, for example, have no corner on beauty or imagination or art, and the sciences have no corner on speculative truth. What is more, a man can be ignorant even of Shakespeare, Aristotle, Beethoven, and Einstein, and be a man for a' that—*if* he has learned how to think his own thoughts, experience beauty for himself, and choose his own actions.

It is not the business of a college to determine or limit what a man will know; if it tries to, he will properly resent its impositions, perhaps immediately, perhaps ten years later when the imposed information is outmoded. But I think that it *is* the business of a college to help teach a man how to use his mind for himself, in at least the three directions I have suggested. There has been a splendid tradition in the College of the University of Chicago of honoring these goals with hard planning and devoted teaching. To think for oneself is, as we all know, hard enough. To design a program and assemble faculty to assist rather than hinder students in their efforts to think for themselves is even harder. But in an age that is oppressed by huge accumulations of unassimilated knowledge, the task of discovering what it means to educate a man is perhaps more important than ever before.

RETURNING COALS
TO NEWCASTLE

F. Champion Ward

To one who can say, "I, too, once lived in Arcady," a return to this university must be marked by trepidation as well as pleasure. There is an exile's duty to give some accounting of years spent in outer darkness. I hope to fulfil this pious obligation in the course of these remarks. There is also apprehension that the light one remembers so gratefully may have flickered or even gone out. With the exception of a few xenophiles, anthropologists, and specialists in intercultural rapport, most Americans overseas become visionary about their own country and its institutions. Exasperated by novel obstructions abroad, they forget the familiar frustrations of home. Private citizens who have rarely wrestled with their own government, they find the government of their new hosts deplorably bureaucratic.

For me, during these *Wanderjahren*, the University of Chicago has remained the place where you will be asked one more question than elsewhere, where tweeds and courtesy never stand in the way of disagreement, where intellect, as the entertainment of possibilities, and intelligence, as the attempt to realize them, set the tone of the community; in short, where theory is taken seriously and made the measure of practice. This university seems always to have had educators who believe that foreign and domestic policies, and even educational systems, ought to derive from clear and distinct ends that practice should do its utmost to realize. As "establishment thinking" widens and dilutes the American consensus, and professors in and out of government can barely remember where they are, a university whose professors do not preshrink their ideas and bevel their thoughts to fit smoothly into prepared policy positions is of great national value. For without such universities and professors there will be neither time nor place for the thorough elaboration of new possibilities; old policies will outlast their occasions; and practice, left to mere practitioners, will be doomed to repeat itself inanely for lack of defined alternatives.

That the University of Chicago still harbors such members was suggested by periodic visits in India from a number of former colleagues, each bent on errands out of the ordinary or managing to place the ordinary in original perspective. One economist of this university was asked by the members of the national planning commission what they might do to encourage the economic development of the country. His rumored reply was simple but drastic: "Gentlemen, disband!" Another colleague, in the course of his study of East Indian intellectuals, succeeded in adding two new subcastes to Indian society: Intellectuals Class A, whom he had interviewed himself, and Intellectuals-Class B, who were interviewed by his assistant.

But was this only an afterglow? Were these visitors also exiles? Definite assurance that Arcady is still Arcady came only when Dean Booth called me up in June, 1965, and invited me to address myself on the present occasion to no less a question than "What knowledge is of most worth?" I knew then that the university had not changed its spots, that it retained its habit of putting forth the most drastic possible questions. I also knew that I was in trouble. This is the one place in the world where it would be most difficult to put forward an original answer to such a question, but it is also the place where it is least possible to dismiss it as unanswerable, undemocratic, and likely to disturb existing arrangements.

Is the question unanswerable? Certainly it was answered often enough in the past, and not by Herbert Spencer only. Gurus and sages in the East, and philosophers, psychologists, and educators in the West have answered it, and debased versions of their solutions have persisted for long periods of time, like undated fossils, embedded in spiritual regimens and in school or university curricula. Sometimes an answer has been found in a belief in a scale of Being which defined the highest knowledge as the knowledge of the highest objects. Sometimes the right guardianship of the state, the saving of the individual soul, or the taming of nature by man have been the ends that determined the worth assigned to different kinds of knowledge. Sometimes knowledge has been viewed as most worthy when most exemplary of what true knowledge ought to be. At other times, rigor has yielded to relevance, and that knowledge has been thought most worthy which served directly the most urgent human concerns.

But perhaps the question is an undemocratic one and thus not answerable in our time. Certainly, an answer came more readily when the worthiest knowledge was that which society reserved for the most worthy few. The plebian societies of the present age, prefigured since De Toqueville's time by our own, have given a more and more spacious reply to the question, "Who is worthy to know?" In the process, as the brahmins, samurai, and nobles of yesterday have been displaced by Everyman, the question, "What is most worth knowing?" has become more and more vexatious. For when faced with questions of relative importance, democratic educators have become adept at pointing out the dangers of reaching agreement, the comforts of unexamined pluralism, and the derangements in store if some policies and practices are found to be better than others. (As if one could not seek the one best curriculum without claiming to have found it, without denying freedom to other seekers, and without confusing a curriculum with a metaphysics.)

This modern reluctance to be clear is more than a simple expression of gregariousness. It has more impressive grounds in the unique aspirations and requirements of modern societies and the resources now available to meet them. To borrow Whitehead's shorthand, modern societies must meet the necessities imposed upon them by "Steam" and by "Democracy." Steam requires an ever higher level of skill and specialized knowledge; democracy requires that whatever is good be shared to the utmost by the many. The knowledge that is of most worth to modern societies, then, is of two apparently competitive kinds, for both of which time, teachers, and facilities must be provided in unprecedented amounts. No wonder that hard-pressed modern educators are reluctant to distinguish these two ends and nourish the hope that the direct pursuit of one will indirectly secure the other.

This duality of ends may be seen, writ large, in the new nations and changing societies of Asia, Africa, and Latin America. To serve as an American educational consultant overseas is to learn not only about other systems of education but about one's own. This is true in two senses. The systems one observes are in most cases derived from European originals and are often out-of-date versions of those models. And since, whether their politics be representative or authoritarian, most of the states in Africa, Asia, and Latin America are now affected by the spirit of equality and the compulsion to "modernize" which marked American educational growth, they are repeating in large part earlier chapters of our own educational history. As De Toqueville, visiting the new Amer-

ican democracy more than a century ago, could say to
Europe, "This is how it will be with us," so the Westerner,
visiting the Third World today, can say, "This is how it was
with us." Second, one comes to view with a fresh eye the
powers and limitations of the present American system as a
model and midwife in helping new societies to enter the age
of Steam and Democracy.

Let us consider more closely what the American educational advisor encounters overseas and what he brings to that
encounter. His ordeal is likely to pass through three stages.
Upon arrival, he often knows about the country only that it
needs many things, including (and this is heady wine) advice
from him. He is apt to be ignorant of its educational system,
since he did not expect to find one at all, and he may be
repelled by his first glimpses of that system and by the
strange idiom and haughty airs of the local elite who are its
products. Therefore, his first impulse is to tear it all up and
start over, preferably with something familiar, like a land-
grant college or a comprehensive high school. When circumstances are particularly favorable to this first and simple
impulse, as they were during the American occupation of
Japan, the full punishment of a fallen foe may include the
whole educational system of the conqueror, complete with
junior high schools and junior colleges, locally elected school
boards, and even the P.T.A.

The advisor's confidence in his dismissal of traditional education is strengthened by the expectations of his hosts, who
tend to regard all Americans as uncouth but temporarily
necessary. They have acquired this view from listening to co-
lonialists and watching tourists. They take it for granted that
Americans will deplore "literary" culture and prescribe "practical" education as its cure. In large part, American consultants have obliged. (Never have I praised manual labor more

or done less of it than during my four years in India.) To help these new nations enter the Age of Steam, the United States has supplied manpower experts, planning economists, technical and vocational specialists, agriculturalists, testers, measurers, and other experts of many kinds, energetic and earnest, uncritical, and not always entirely "couth." And in spite of enormous obstacles and handicaps at home and abroad, a very great deal has been accomplished, particularly in the last few years, as trained manpower and training facilities have reached "critical" numbers in some fields and places.

But many American educational prescriptions have not followed strictly from a calculation of economic needs. Americans have also urged universal literacy, the rapid expansion of secondary education, talent searches and scholarships for poor students, techniques for handling masses of university students, and even the encouragement of native arts. To give them and their authors a hard-bitten air, these proposals are often clothed in the idiom of economics or politics. Any amount or kind of education may be loosely defended as an "investment in human resources," or it may be said to be politically "explosive" to withhold education from young people who want it or to give it to those (often, alas, the same young people) who are likely to be out of work. But, at bottom, for American advisors these prescriptions are articles of faith, deeply democratic assertions of the rightness of educating every person, not because of his economic value or political influence, but because of his dignity as a human being and his rights as a citizen.

The most directly liberal of all American educational exports is the notion of a common higher learning which at bottom is neither elitist nor vocational. Many societies have believed that some knowledge is of most worth, but that most learners were not worthy of it. So far as higher education is concerned, they have accepted the contention of Nietzsche that to speak of a "common good" is to contradict oneself. The idea of a common *lower* learning is accepted even among robins, who teach all their young to fly. All modern societies also accept the idea of higher uncommon or specialized learning. It remained for America to press home the idea of a higher common learning extending beyond the level of schooling, and, theoretically, to everyone. In his admirable book, *The Search for a Common Learning* (New York: McGraw-Hill, 1962), Russell Thomas has shown how this idea has haunted American higher education, now shaping its course as a positive aim, now tugging reproachfully at the helmsman's conscience when other courses were set, now dismissed as an impracticable and indeed coercive principle, now viewed as a universal right and social necessity.

The history of the University of Chicago illustrates the career of this idea with unusual vividness. Because of the seriousness with which theory has been taken at this university, the vicissitudes of what has here been called "general, higher education" have been more plangent than elsewhere and they have been accompanied by an instructive oscillation between the exhilaration of pioneering and the occasional sheer relief of not searching for a higher common learning any more strenuously than anyone else.

This American idea of a widely shared wisdom now also haunts the world. In one form or another, it is receiving its first test in universities in Asia and Latin America, and it has even been given a cautious trial in some of the British universities, ancient, middle-aged, and new. American advisors have played active roles in many of these endeavors. In so doing, they have expressed most directly and ambitiously America's commitment to Democracy as well as to Steam.

But this takes us into the second stage of our American consultant's experience abroad. As befits a second act, this stage is marked by complications and the general puzzlement of our hero. The complications arise from two sources: the existing system in the country the American consultant is attempting to assist, and the tensions and discrepancies he finds in his bag of prescriptions. The local system turns out to be both more persistent and more versatile than he had first supposed. On the one hand, the elite of the country, although they give verbal and even sincere agreement to the reform of the system that produced them, find it difficult, in fact, to rend their own nest. They are apt to agree that the *village* people should have a new kind of education, but they are careful to insure that their own progeny are educated in the very tradition which they have agreed to reform. On the other hand, the existing system turns out, under labels that were unfamiliar to our advisor, to have been attempting to provide a number of the forms of practical training that he had thought were neglected altogether. He is forced to concede, for example, that adults may actually be educated by agencies called "extra-mural departments" and that secondary schools may be influenced usefully by "institutes of education." He also may find that the colonial past is strewn with attempts to get Africans and Asians to patronize farm institutes, technical schools, and other colonial centers of practical education, and that there are even records of colonial district officers having to spend much of their time persuading Asian and African parents to let their children go to school at all.

Had the solidarity of NATO extended to its educators, some of these naïve shocks might have been avoided, to the distinct benefit of the new nations. The first *lycée* I ever entered was not in France but in Turkey, where it was spelled *lise,* and I have visited more institutes of education in Africa than in England. Here I must pay tribute to the Carnegie Corporation, which supported Alan Pifer and Stephen Stackpole in bringing together British and American educators before the latter had become fully active in former British Africa. These meetings spared the Africans at least some of the divided counsel and blind repetition of sad experience that would have been visited upon them otherwise. Tribute must also be paid to the British. With that resiliency that insures that there will always be an England, Britishers long familiar with African educational development spent little time in sulking over a lost grandeur. They set about willingly to marry their experience to American ideas and money in order that (to adapt Churchill's wartime plea) the old former colonies, in all their power and might, might come to the rescue of the new. It is one of the few cases in which educators of two "developed" countries have attempted to consult together before ministering to the patient.

Along with this growing complication in his response to the limitations and capabilities of the existing system, our advisor is further sobered by the uneasy mixture of instrumental and liberal nostrums his own system has provided him. Under the pressure of fiscal limitations obtaining in the new countries, obscurities which he has been able to leave more or less unexamined at home become pointed and troublesome abroad. Above all, Robert Hutchins' trenchant question, "Must democracy mean that everyone is entitled to a bad education?" haunts and plagues the advisor's mind and conscience. If, for example, not everyone can be educated, should as many as possible be educated somehow, or should a Jeffersonian approach be adopted and equality be sought only in the form of equal *access* by the talented few to a system small enough to be good? Should the mass media be resorted to in order to maximize literacy and useful knowlege, or should such investments be resisted, on the ground that critical, independent, individual minds are the first requirement of a free society? Should manpower planning be carried to the point where career choices are not made by individual students but by planners allocating them to quotas of "high-level manpower"?

Again, what do we Westerners assume when we deride the fact that at an African university the first chair established was in classics? Our usual response is, "This is not what 'these people' need." Does this mean that the Free World shares with its global adversary the view that prosperity comes before freedom? Are the humanities to be cultivated only in affluent societies? Is steam the precursor of democracy? Would New England have flowered on that hypothesis? Would Harvard have been established when it was?

At this point, our consultant has entered the third phase, in which he is likely to remain. I am afraid that no neat *dénouement* marks this third act. Rather, a mood of chastened eclecticism sets in. The advisor accepts both the spotted actuality of what he finds in being and of what he brings with him from the United States. If his temper is sanguine, as it usually is, he may even display that exuberant fatalism with which we Americans embrace large, shapeless trends and help to make them larger. He decides to take only short views, to do what he can, starting where and when he can, and then "taking it from there."

A foundation executive may be somewhat unkindly defined as a eunuch consoled by gold. As such, I suppose that I should have accepted quite comfortably eclecticism in practice and inconsistency in theory. Indeed, there is no escaping a considerable opportunism in educational as well as economic development, and I have indulged in my full share of it. But once an Arcadian, always an Arcadian. I am afraid that my own chastening abroad has served to deepen a conviction that I acquired somewhat strenuously at this university, that the structure of educational systems has much to do with what can be accomplished by them, and that, although there is indeed more than one way to skin a cat, in certain educational systems some important cats are simply left unskinned.

The recent history of the first degree course in Indian universities affords an example of this interplay of structure and achievement in higher education. Twelve years ago, when I was first in India, a major effort was made to change the arrangements for post-secondary education. In most Indian universities, these had consisted of a two-year "intermediate" program followed by a first degree course of two years. To shift some of this load back to the high schools, so that students would come later and in smaller numbers to the university, thus enabling the university departments to concentrate on coherent courses of study in single subjects, the "intermediate" program was dropped and the first degree course of three years' duration was adopted by most of the Indian universities. Shortly after this decision was reached, on the basis of recommendations made in the Radhakrishnan report on university education, India decided to look into the possibility of incorporating into the university program general studies that looked not to the specialized prospects of individual students, but to their common membership in the leadership of their country and in the human race. One of the first obstacles encountered was how to incorporate general studies in a degree course modeled on the British tradition of specialized study at the university level. Again, a major effort has been made, and some general education is now a part of the programs of many Indian universities. But there is a familiar ring about the difficulties being encountered. One hears of prefixing a "transitional" year to the present university course to provide more time for general studies, of the difficulties of getting the faculties to carry on general, higher education, and of the problem of convincing the students (against all the evidence) that their general education is regarded as no less important than their departmental work.

In Latin America, a number of the leading universities have been adopting programs of general studies designed to give a common learning to students before they enter different professional faculties and to bring together in departments the work of specialists in single disciplines now scattered through several faculties. As Izaak Wirszup of this university has discerned in the case of Colombia, the looming problem in these universities is to develop and teach common courses rigorous enough to satisfy the departments that are responsible for them and relevant enough to satisfy the professional faculties that the students will seek to attend.

Some years ago, in a provincial government of a large African state, an attempt by an American-educated African leader to introduce universal primary education failed for lack of funds, and the resulting frustrated hopes, particularly those of the mothers of students of primary age, brought down the government. At that time, there was only one university in the country, with seats for fewer than one thousand students.

These examples of syncretism in education, even when the reservoir from which elements and ideas are drawn includes the United States, the United Kingdom, and Europe, are enough to show that opportunism in the development of educational systems is not enough. Systematic deliberation concerning educational development is required, and it cannot escape the consideration of ends as well as means. I have come to believe that such deliberation must include three levels, phases, or modes, which I shall call the reflective, the calculative, and the operative. I would like to say a word about each of these.

The reflective mode might also be called "reflexive" or even "philosophical," for I have in mind attempts to identify and clarify basic general assumptions about political and social purposes and values and the tensions between such assumptions that often guide (or infect) educational planning in its calculative and operative modes. We all know in a general way that national purposes and social traditions may conflict with each other or with those of the most right-minded foreign consultant. But the degree of attention paid to these assumptions and their mutual relations has varied greatly in actual educational planning in the last fifteen years. In a few cases, the ends of education may be explicitly formulated in their relation to national goals and translated with care into allocations and programs. More often, however, ends have been vaguely subscribed to but neither traced out carefully in terms of their consequences for investment nor reflected in the actual forms taken by educational institutions and activities.

Let me illustrate this point again from the case of India. In 1957, on being asked by an educational journal to look back over three years' observation of Indian educational development, I was led to characterize Indian educational thought in terms of certain "ideal polarities which supply the terms in which possible programs and institutions are being explored and defined." [1] These polarities may now serve to illustrate the reflective mode of educational planning. One of them, perhaps the most pervasive, was that of the few and the many, generated by the attempt of the "Sovereign Demo-

---

[1] *Phi Kappa Lambda*, December, 1957, p. 108.

cratic Republic of India" deliberately to convert itself from
an aristocracy into a democracy. This immense national commitment was, of course, accepted with every degree of clarity
and conviction, from high seriousness and dedicated effort,
through lip service, to outright resistance and charges of blas-
phemy against the constitutional provision abolishing un-
touchability. In education, this commitment has affected a
wide range of matters, from the reallocation of university
scholarships in favor of "scheduled castes" to the rapid opening of village schools. It has stimulated the expansion of
education while impairing its quality.

A second polarity illustrates the tension that may arise
when national ends are accepted selectively by distinct groups
which hold different purposes for the society. I refer to the set
of differences centering around India's interest in traditional
crafts, basic schools, and rural institutes, on the one hand,
and industry, technical training, and engineering on the other.
In India much more than elsewhere, this issue was "complicated and deepened by allegiance to the life and thought of
Mahatma Gandhi. Gandhi refused to look upon the villager
and village life as simply deficient in the goods, services, and
amenities which large factories and large cities can supply.
Like Jefferson, he saw a special virtue in agrarian life, and he
wanted rural benefits of all kinds planned in such a way as to
reinforce the rural virtues, not to supplant or corrupt them." [2]

On the other side of this issue have been most foreign
consultants and urban, educated Indians bent on modernizing India after the model of Western societies. Thus, the
deepest values that the father of Indian independence hoped
that independence would bring to the fore in Indian life have
been faced with new competitors arising from India's economic and social evolution since 1947. The issue is by no

[2] *Ibid.,* p. 109.

means resolved and continues to affect the discussion, support, and conduct of education in India.

Those familiar with the Muslim and African worlds will cite their own examples of the influence on education of national assumptions concerning the social and political ends which the educational system is expected to help the nation to realize. The continuing interplay, in Turkey and Egypt, between traditional Islamic values and the modernizing ideas of Kemal Ataturk and Gamal Abdul Nasser is an obvious example.

At present, it is the calculative mode of educational planning that, thanks in large part to Theodore Schultz of this university, is most in vogue. It has to do with allocation and choice in the investment of resources for educational development, and, I would add, with the optimal distribution of students and teachers at different educational levels. It attempts to make estimates of the relative returns to be expected from different amounts and rates of investment in education and describes that investment by numbers and categories of persons selected, educated or trained, and then put to work. Its tools are manpower planning and economic analysis.

Thanks to the new interest in such calculative planning, education has at least improved its rhetorical position as a putative source of economic development. In the 1950's, education was still viewed by most ministries of finance and planning commissions as a social service, awkwardly popular with the people and hence with the politicians. It was given only residual attention in national development plans. Also, it was some years before manpower planning for economic development was sufficiently advanced and accepted to affect the autochthonous planning, such as estimating the number of teachers needed for a burgeoning elementary school system, which always goes on within education ministries. Studies of educational problems were produced by "educationists" only, and the economist appeared only in the pale form of a "coster" or a watchdog from "Finance." At the same time, economic development plans were drawn up almost exclusively by groups of economists, who looked upon "educationists" as one group of special pleaders for increased allocations.

It was only about five years ago that the view of education as a factor of production, deserving the status of a form of investment, began to affect educational planning. The first important fruit of this change of viewpoint was the "Ashby Commission" report, *Investment in Education,* which was submitted to the government of Nigeria in 1960. There, a former University of Chicago economist managed to get on board and, in the absence of a national economic plan (at that time still in preparation), projected a certain growth rate for the economy and connected it to the development of the educational system by means of estimates of the economy's future needs for highly skilled manpower. It is not possible to prove this statement, but I believe that the scale of support to education which the Ashby Commission recommended was considerably larger because of the approach taken than it would have been at the hands of the traditional commission of educationists. The contrast is striking between the dour presence of the traditional figure from the ministry of finance, pointing out that education must be restricted because resources are limited, and the modern "development economist," pointing out that resources will continue to be limited unless education is expanded.

Finally, I would distinguish the operative mode of educational planning. This is the familiar level of specific educational structures, programs, institutions, and methods, which are judged to be most likely to secure the ends identified and subscribed to in the reflective mode, within the quotas estimated and the resources committed in the calculative mode.

To my mind, a chief lesson of the last fifteen years is provided by the large number of mutually insulated activities on the various levels distinguished above and the relatively few cases in which what is done at the operative level is fully consistent with the outcomes of planning in the reflective and calculative modes. It is not surprising that this should be the case. Quite apart from the pressures and distractions affecting the educators of a particular country, each foreign consultant or agency brings into the country distinct and unevenly developed philosophical assumptions, bases of calculation, and operational models. In fact, these are often deposited by distinct species of experts, often dealing with separate elements in the host country. The result is too many cases of social purposes left unexamined until calculations and operations run into unexpected obstacles, educational structures not appropriate to their content, financial allocations not consistent with social ends or operational capacities, and operations reflecting alien purposes or costing too much money.

Reflection on such cases suggest that a more inclusive conception of planning would be of real value to educational development everywhere. Educational consultants should in the future have at least a degree of capability in all three modes of planning, and the ability, even though a variety of specialists are engaged at particular points in a given educational activity, to define and maintain a frame of reference for the development as a whole which extends beyond the boundaries of any particular phase or part.

I spoke just now of the benefits of planning to educational development everywhere. Everywhere includes our own country. But must the physician heal himself, or is it only the poor who must plan? Our present national provision for education, our "system," is not the product of planning but of frequent borrowings, occasional inventions, and sustained accretion. It has not yet bankrupted the country, and its major components—schools, colleges, and universities—continue to display considerable staying-power. Therefore, should not American education remain the unmoved mover of the educational world, exempt from that clarification of ends and economy of means which modernization and penury now require of developing countries?

If all were placid progress at the present time, it would be visionary to urge that the American educational system would gain from a greater degree of deliberation concerning its effectiveness as a system of ends and means. The statement would be true, but no such deliberation would occur. We have been isolated and rich enough to be vague about ends and lavish about means. Here and there, single institutions, or even single communities or states, have altered the length or function of this or that segment of the system, but such innovations tend to be self-isolating. They are less often imitated than deplored, and their sponsors, unconvinced perhaps but bruised and lonely, sooner or later decide to get back in line. It is true that some universities retain at least one novel feature, the product of some extraordinary effort by an individual or minority who once drove quickly into a momentary opening in the wall of academic convention. But these venerable novelties only prove the rule. They survive through their very uniqueness as one-time experiments. They perform a double service. They prove that the university which conceived them is a forward-looking place. They thus make further innovations unnecessary.

But "placid progress" hardly describes the present educational scene in the United States. From Sputnik to Berkeley, it has been a time of unusual stress concerning the quality of high school science teaching, the special requirements of the socially disadvantaged, the neglect of undergraduate education, the new strains on the four-year college, the rise in the level of education and skills needed for employment, and the expansion of federal support of education.

These stresses have appeared at a succession of points in the American educational structure, beginning in the 1950's in the high school, when it rediscovered rigor and the superior student, then in the college, as it received the precocious and the well-prepared, then in the early and preschool years of education, as the disadvantaged fell behind, and then, as the New Frontier and the Great Society spread their wings, in the web of traditional relationships among federal, state, and church resources and responsibilities. Although the first impact of each of these stresses has been restricted, repercussions in other parts of the system have accumulated so rapidly that even a former president of Harvard University has called for "shaping educational policy" on a national basis by means of an "interstate commission." My fellow speaker at this conference, Governor Sanford, is even now engaged in making that commission a reality. I am sure that anyone who has had to describe, explain, and exploit our educational system in other countries will welcome this interstate effort to get beyond the folklore of localism. For what is striking about the American system is that localism rarely induces the creativity so often claimed for it. Educational differences among the states are almost entirely differences of better and worse among similar types of institutions, arranged in very much the same sequence and pattern in each state. Thus, we have the paradox that a system purporting to insure variety and experimental flexibility remains basically uniform. It is simply harder to change deliberately than centralized systems are and more subject to enduring qualitative discrepancies.

Thus, a poor but bright boy in the backward regions of France has a better chance of being well educated than does such a boy in the United States, and he is rather more likely to become an individualist.

Let us select for closer examination the current efforts of the American educational system to provide that shared wisdom which was cited earlier as a characteristically American article of faith and educational export. As various American advisors commended it abroad, hów has the higher common learning been faring at home? To this Rip van Winkle, it seems increasingly clear that of the two great ends of modern education, Steam has been gaining over Democracy. The demands of an increasingly sophisticated economy and a highly competitive world role have given pride of place to the *sine qua non* of skilled manpower. At the same time, however, the growing need for wisdom, for versatility of judgment, and for wide and sophisticated communication remains obvious. To be a business executive, a scholar or scientist, or a civil servant, diplomat, or politician requires a range of informed response that grows wider daily.

After ten years' absence, I recently "moderated" an "executives' session" in Aspen. The most striking change I observed was in the recognition by modern executives that business decisions now must take into account a greatly widened range of social facts and values. Overseas, it has also become clear to highly specialized economists, educationists, and political scientists attempting to be useful to developing countries that single modes of analysis do not provide adequate ground for a wide range of policy decisions. We are discovering too that if East and West, North and South, are to meet rather than collide, the education of at least the elites of all countries must in some way become universal. Thus, at a point in history when there is the strongest of cases for instilling, more seriously and thoroughly than ever before, a common higher learning in the rising generation everywhere, there is widespread uncertainty in our own country as to how, when, and where to do it.

To date, the bifocal, four-year college has provided the principal setting wherein American education seeks to achieve its two great ends. Yet its attempt to juxtapose two-thirds of a general education and two-thirds of a master's program in a single course of study appears to be under rather widespread criticism. I have expatiated elsewhere on the strains and lapses that, in my view, inevitably attend the attempt to realize two distinct and principal purposes in a single course of study.

> Because the [bifocal curriculum] culminates in "majors" in single subjects for which academic departments are made responsible, these departments become the principal points of attachment for both students and faculty. As a result, when thus placed in a single degree program with specialized education, general education contracts "to fill the time available." Theoretically, there may be an even division of the four-year course into two halves, but close examination of the half devoted to general education reveals that the two years of work of which it is composed becomes a *pastiche* of survey courses for "non-majors," prerequisites required or suggested by departments and professional associations, and introductions to single subjects. It is almost inevitable that members of a faculty appointed and advanced by departments will give pride of place to departmental interests and expectations. It is predictable, also, that as between general and departmental requirements for a single degree, students will slight the former.[3]

One may cite these and other defects in the existing structure without expecting them to be removed. Indeed, the

[3] *Humanistic Education and Western Civilization* (New York: Holt, Rinehart, and Winston, Inc., 1964), pp. 123–24.

most likely prospect, despite what many critics, and not alone
Jacques Barzun, are saying, is that the traditional structure
will survive once more, principally because, like Mount Ever-
est, "it is there." Yet on this occasion, in this citadel of theory,
it is incumbent upon us to entertain other possibilities that
might give to our society the fullest possible measure of both
shared wisdom and expertise.

I see two major alternatives to the present order. I will first
discuss the one that seems to me to be more likely to succeed
but less likely to be tried. It assigns a specific end to each
segment of the school-college-university sequence central to
American education, and it attempts to be realistic in assessing the powers and limitations of existing American schools,
colleges, and universities actually to realize those ends, and
not simply to claim, or hope, to do so. It is therefore prepared, if this assessment requires it, to disturb existing
arrangements. In short, it recognizes fully the influence that
the log can exercise on both Mark Hopkins and his students.

Let me begin with schooling and return a few more coals
to Newcastle. I have never been able to forget a complaint
that Frank Knight once lodged with me when I was dean of
this university's college. He accused the college of "pander-
ing" to the adolescent's love of general ideas and cited the
confident ignorance of one college student who had referred
spaciously to "Cuba and Manila and all down through
there." I also recall Marshall Stone intervening in a university
senate council review of the Laboratory School's program to
point out that even a student's "social adjustment" may depend crucially on his ability to speak and write clearly and
accurately.

These coals remind us that a bias toward the particular
ought to pervade the work of the schools. I do not mean that
only tidily ordered "layers of facts" should be purveyed or
that facts are intelligible or indeed memorable except in a

context of meaning, but I do plead for an habitual modesty and discipline in the selection of topics and the definition of tasks.

When schooling with such a bias has been successful, the high school graduate will have good writing in his knuckles, so to speak; he will have a foreign language on his tongue; in the arts and music, his eye and his ear will, as Plato put it, prefer the best without knowing why; he will worry and re-shape his statements until their meanings are as precise "as the subject permits"; he will even begin to feel in his bones what it means to make practical judgments, in the dim, un-even light of stubborn facts. In instilling this sense of the particular, the school, in my view, will be functioning at its best. This is what needs most to be done at this stage and it is what the school's leaders, teachers, and communities can most steadily understand, achieve, and support.

If it focuses on this task, I believe that the school can succeed in it by the end of what is now the eleventh year of schooling. I also believe that this is none too soon, for there is further work to do for which adequate time and special auspices must be found. This work is that of the college, defined as that stage at which a higher common learning is instilled in those graduates of the high school who are capa-ble of profiting from it. At this second major stage, ac-quaintance with particulars continues steadily, but analytic, critical, and synoptic activities are increasingly stressed. Learn-ing becomes a quickening rather than a transmission or an exposure. Subjects are studied in terms of the principles on which they rest and the modes of inquiry by which those principles are established.

In the college years, students have a certain generosity of mind and freedom from vocational anxiety that, if the high school has done its job well, can be safely and usefully "pan-dered to." Therefore, the optimal use for the collegiate years is to convince the intelligent young American that "the un-examined life is no life for a man." Since this conviction is more apt to be stilled than instilled during the student's later career, to instill it should be the shaping purpose of a distinct stage of education.

Since the aim of the college is a common education in principles permitting communication and rational progress to occur among citizens otherwise variously expert and occupied, the college program should have the same degree of coherence for its students and teachers as does a course of professional study. In this connection, it is time to return another coal. I believe that this university's uniquely rigorous attempt to realize the idea of general, higher education has already shown that if a higher common learning is to be made the central business of the collegiate stage of American education. the bifocal college should be abandoned in favor of a three-year course of liberal studies under the control of a single faculty of scholarly teachers, grouped in units broader than departments and subject to advancement on the basis of their qualities as educators.

In such a college, the teacher should be skilled above all in teaching. His scholarship should consist in a critical grasp of the subject to be taught, a readiness to relate it to other subjects, and an unforced "production" of interpretative writing. He should exemplify the reflective citizen at the service of learning.

The college should not be superintended, like the high school, or managed, like the university. It should have as its head a president or dean who retains a wistful interest in liberal education which he is encouraged to pursue, a board of trustees, faculty control of the curriculum, and no departments.

Beyond the college would loom the university. It is the

home of specialized and professional learning and of the disciplined but freely directed pursuit of new knowledge and complete understanding. For the better graduates of the college, the university would in the first instance provide three-year courses of study leading to the master's degree, and for the strongest of these masters, doctoral and post-doctoral programs. For other competent students seeking professional degrees, appropriate postcollegiate preparation of varying kinds would be provided.

Thus, in the structure here proposed, the major points of sorting would come at the end of eleven years of schooling, three years of college, and three years of specialized study. Each level of the structure would have a single educational end and an optimal prospect of achieving it. It seems to me clearly better than the present national arrangement of twelve years of schooling, followed by two fragmented years of "lower division" work, followed, for able and mediocre students alike, by two years of undergraduate "concentration," followed by one or two years of "master's" work, often under new management.

If this 11–3–3 structure were to be adopted, some changes in existing arrangements would be required. The subtraction, however, of one year from the period of schooling might prove temporary. Given the rate at which "preschooling" is growing, students may in time begin, as well as end, their schooling sooner than at present.

At the collegiate level, a number of now distinct kinds of institution would become jointly responsible for maintaining for this country a reflective citizenry. They would include the following: first, junior colleges of arts and sciences, which would absorb the present last year of schooling into a three-year course, *not* to be described or conceived as the twelfth, thirteenth, and fourteenth grades. Second would be the large category of four-year independent and university colleges, which would reduce their first course of study by one year. Of these, those having limited resources would confine themselves to common higher learning and those that are stronger would also award the master's degree, with emphasis—especially in the stronger independent colleges—upon the preparation of high school and college teachers. Third, the possibility should be explored that some of the best of our preparatory schools might become colleges sending their abler graduates to the university, ready, as in Europe, to pursue specialized courses of study.

An appropriate structure is, I believe, a crucial condition if our national educational effort is to meet the equal and distinct demands of Steam and Democracy. The failure to recognize this necessity has been a major recurrent cause of educational ineffectiveness. But an appropriate structure does not insure good quality; it only makes it possible. In the case of the system here proposed, I believe that some of the lessons learned in recent years in connection with the improvement of high school science and mathematics should be applied to the college program. Universities should be devoted primarily to specialized learning, but they should take a continuing interest in the good health and progress of the colleges surrounding them or affiliated with them. This interest should be expressed in three principal ways. First, although the mass of college students would be elsewhere, each major university should maintain a college of its own as an experimental model of what can be done. Second, leading university scholars and scientists should be available to the colleges periodically, not as classroom teachers, but as counselors, critics, and trustees, in insuring the authenticity and quality of the common higher learning presented in the colleges.

Finally, the university should regularly be host to members of the faculties of surrounding colleges, both in connection with the role of the university's own college as a source of light and in order to give regular opportunities to the members of surrounding colleges to study and work in their subjects during summers and sabbatical leaves.

The result of such a relationship between universities and the colleges of their areas would be neither complete pluralism nor a national curriculum, but a limited pluralism seeking to combine variety with good standards.

(At this point, you will be relieved if I remind you that my writ as a Ford Foundation executive does not run on this continent. Therefore, any resemblance between what I have been advocating and what is likely to be supported by my foundation is unlikely.)

The variant of existing practice which seems more likely to be tried, in America and overseas, attempts a change of content within the established structure. For most students, a four-year first degree course is retained, but the division of that course into lower and upper divisions or halves is not retained. General studies no longer constitute even a truncated whole at the level of the college; at the same time, specialized studies are broadened to become to some extent divisional rather than departmental in scope.

The importance of general education to any modern society is not denied by the proponents of this variant. Therefore, it is clear that they are optimistic about two matters concerning which I have already expressed some doubts. These are the capacity of our high schools to take over and conduct at a good standard those general studies which have been heretofore the responsibility of the lower division of the college, and the capacity of university faculties to organize themselves in such a way as to plan and regularly teach undergraduate programs not confined to single departments or mere aggregates thereof.

In a minority of our high schools, at the hands of some teachers, it has already been demonstrated that some subjects (most frequently mathematics, the sciences, music, and the creative arts) can be presented at a level that is challenging to even the best high school students. Inventive efforts to develop a similar capacity in other subjects are now being made. It is likely that, despite the unscholarly atmosphere surrounding public education and the restiveness and precocity of high school students, further successes will be scored. These are all to the good, and if they do become general rather than exceptional, they will make very good sense of the idea that the first university course should be centered in a particular division of cognate subjects, selected by the student on the basis of an intellectual bent discovered in high school. The result would be a pyramidal sequence, extending from a study of all subjects in high school, through a division of studies in college, to single subjects at the doctoral and professional levels.

Before his death last summer, Dean William DeVane anticipated these tendencies by making the case for divisional studies at the first degree level, perhaps on the general model of Oxford's Modern Greats. A recent visit to one of the new British universities suggests that they have left even Modern Greats behind and, indeed, are setting the pace for the English-speaking world. Moreover, since they are new and passing from narrowness to breadth, while American universities are old and passing from breadth to greater concentration, there is a verve and sense of discovery in these English universities not yet matched on this side of the Atlantic.

The new universities in Britain have also been mindful of the pitfalls that await attempts to combine breadth of curriculum with departmental organization. Their adoption of the school of studies rather than the department as not only the basic unit of study for students but as the primary administrative unit and point of attachment for faculty members is a recognition of that interdependence of structure and accomplishment in education which is my principal theme today. If the new curricula are to be steadily successful, here or in Great Britain, and not merely interesting episodes for scholars and scientists whose primary obligations lie elsewhere, something like these British arrangements will be essential.

From reading and conversation, I have learned that this university, as befits a Chicago institution, is now setting out to recapture the blue ribbon from the British. I understand that the possibilities of divisional colleges and divisional courses of study are being explored. Since I am here today to return coals, not to rake them over, I will restrain a first and reactionary impulse to find a self-contradiction in the idea of a divisional college. Instead, I am glad, indeed, to learn of this prospect and only wish that I could have contributed in detail today to your specifications of this idea. As a rusty and nostalgic Arcadian, I can only welcome your undertaking and express once more the hope that whatever may in theory be thought most worthy of being taught and learned here will, in fact, be taught and learned. To insure this, I now believe, requires direct and candid attention to the overall structure as well as the professed aims of the American educational system, to the sociology of academic careers in the United States, and to the optimal definition and interplay of school, college, and university.

THE INSTRUMENTS OF
MENTAL PRODUCTION

Northrop Frye

I have chosen a slightly different approach from the question assigned—"What Knowledge Is Most Worth Having?" —because, like everybody else, I want to quarrel with assumptions in that question. In the first place, the knowledge of most worth, whatever it may be, is not something one has: it is something one is, and the correct response to such a question, if a student were to ask it, would be another question—"With what body of knowledge do you wish to identify yourself?" In the second place, the phrase "most worth" is apt to introduce comparative value judgments into areas where they are irrelevant. Whenever students ask me if I would advise them to "take" sociology or anthropology, ancient history or modern history, a science option or a language option, I realize that there are no objective answers, and no possible means of arriving at any. The answer depends on what criteria they adopt, but not on anything in the structure of knowledge itself that I or anyone else can demonstrate to them. I suppose there is such a thing as practically and inherently useless knowledge, that is, subjects without content or founded on false assumptions, like palmistry or the racial theories cherished by the Nazis; but the danger of a student's being deflected by them is remote. The knowledge of most worth, for a genuine student, is that body of knowledge to which he has already made an unconscious commitment. I speak of an unconscious commitment because for a genuine student, knowledge, like marriage, is too important a matter to be left entirely to conscious choice.

Conscious choice is for the uncommitted, and for those the standards employed in the choice can come only from various factors in their own lives, such as a picture of one's future career, a sense of what one is good at, a guess about the market value of one kind of knowledge as compared with another, or simply the kind of instinctive preference that it is not really necessary to rationalize.

I begin by separating general education and scholarship, which are not integrally connected. Intellectually, the world is specialized and pluralistic, and learning, like the amoeba, can reproduce only by subdividing. One may organize colloquia around general topics like communication, and get Romance philologists and solid-state physicists to "communicate" with each other in an unsubstantial Eucharist. Scholars may do this kind of thing under pressure, but for the most part they will do it dutifully, like voting, and not with the exhilaration that they would get from discussing their own specialization with some of the very few people in the world who share it. Actual scholarship is esoteric, almost conspiratorial, and the principles of academic freedom require that it should be left that way. The scholar *qua* scholar is responsible only to his subject. Students should not try to "evaluate" him as a public performer in the classroom; administrators and private foundations should not harass him by telling him that he ought to learn more about different fields; journalists and politicians should not repeat silly clichés like "ivory tower" to describe his intellectual home. In an age when the word "dialogue" has acquired so potent a charge of verbal magic, it is worth reminding ourselves that in Plato, who seems to have invented the conception, dialogue exists solely for the purpose of destroying false knowledge. As soon as any genuine knowledge (or what Plato regarded as such) is present, the dialogue turns into a punctuated monologue. What the world of scholarship requires is not two but at least a hundred and two cultures, all more or less unintelligible to one another, and the improvement of scholarship is toward more and not fewer.

What I have just described is the *routine* of scholarship only. Its patron saint is Sherlock Holmes, who never failed to solve any problem put before him because of the purity of his dedication to scholarship. Sherlock Holmes rather resented the fact that Watson had never read his little monograph on the distinguishing of 140 varieties of cigar ash, but when Watson told him that the earth was a globe revolving around the sun, he remarked that that was an irrelevant piece of information that he would do his best to forget. But of course many other things go on as well as the routine of scholarship, notably a process of mutation and metamorphosis. Subjects regroup themselves and other subjects take shape from the shifting relations of existing ones, as geophysics takes shape from a new relation of geology and physics. It is in these moments of regrouping that the great genius, with his colossal simplifying vision, gets his best chance to emerge. I wonder if anyone of Freud's stature could emerge from psychology now: there might be a feeling that he was an armchair theorist who had not served enough time in laboratory routine to be a proper professional psychologist. The Freuds of the future are more likely to emerge, as Freud himself did, from a point of mutation at which psychology begins to turn into something unrecognizable to its scholarly establishment. But these mutations occur from within existing disciplines at a certain stage in their inner development: they cannot be planned or even directly encouraged from the outside.

General education is a social and not primarily an intellectual matter, and has no authority over productive scholarship. All discussion of it must be related to the state of society and the needs, desires, and ideals of that society. There is a body of information and skill that everybody has to know and possess in order to participate in our complex society, and the question is how far up, subjectively in life and objectively in the structure of knowledge, such a body extends, or can profitably be extended. We may assume that we can distinguish two levels in general education: an average or elementary level and a cultivated level; roughly, the difference between being able to read and write and being able to read with some depth and direction and write with some articulateness. At present many believe that raising people to the cultivated level on a huge and unprecedented scale is not merely desirable in itself but a necessity if our civilization is to survive. There has always been a practical distinction between what is important, like cathedrals, and what is necessary, like privies: in our day the important seems, possibly for the first time in history, to be becoming necessary as well.

Ever since Adam was thrown out of Paradise and told to go and till an accursed ground, the most important distinction in human life has been the distinction between labor and leisure. By labor, here, I mean the whole productive aspect of society, the accumulating and distributing of food and the means of shelter and the more specific wants of a settled social order. According to what is perhaps the most famous book ever written at the University of Chicago, Adam soon tires of tilling the ground and compels Eve to do it instead, confining his own activities to hunting and fishing and thereby beginning a "leisure class," the class that is defined as superior because it contributes nothing to social production. When leisure and labor become personified as an upper and a lower class, the conceptions of waste and alienation come into society: alienation for the worker, who is cheated out of nearly all the fruit of his own labor, and waste for the leisurely consumer, who can put nothing to productive use. American democracy has blurred these social distinctions and has replaced the leisure class with the affluent society, but it has not thereby lessened the feelings of waste and alienation. The sense that society, considered in its producing and distributing aspect, is something cheap and ignoble, that it is not worth loyalty, that many of its products are absurdities and that operating its obsessively busy machinery is spiritually futile, is at least as strong as it ever was. And this time there is nobody to hate, no tyrants or silk-hatted capitalists or swaggering lords, no one essentially different from ourselves whom we can relieve our feelings by abusing.

In a society devoted wholly to labor, leisure would be thought of as merely rest or spare time: If there is continuous leisure, it becomes idleness or distraction. Idleness and distraction are reactions against the unpleasantness or dullness of labor: they make up for the time wasted on work by wasting time in other ways. A life divided only between dull work and distracted play is not life but essentially a mere waiting for death, and war comes to such a society as a deliverance, because it relieves the strain of waiting. It is generally realized that idleness and distraction are very close to the kind of boredom that expresses itself in smashing things, and hence there is a widespread feeling, which is at least a century old, that mass education is needed simply to keep people out of mischief. This is not a very inspiring philosophy of education, nor one at all likely to effect its purposes.

Education has nothing to do with this vicious circle of labor and idleness: it begins in that moment of genuine leisure in which Adam is neither tilling the ground nor going fishing and leaving the real work to Eve, but remembering his lost Paradise. Even as late as Milton, articulating the dream of a lost Paradise is still the definition of education. More prosaically, we may say that education is the product of a vision of human society that is more permanent and coherent than actual society. When the students of today were babies, the King of England was emperor of India, China was a bourgeois friend, Japan a totalitarian enemy, and Nazi Germany was ruling as powerful an empire as the world had ever seen. It is clear that what we think of as real society is not that at all, but only the transient appearance of society. A society in which the presidency of the United States can be changed by one psychotic with a rifle is not sufficiently real for any thoughtful person to want to live wholly within it. What real society is, is indicated by the structure of the arts and sciences in a university. This is the permanent body of what humanity has done and is still doing, and the explanations of why the world around us changes so suddenly and so drastically are to be found only there.

A theory of education, then, implies a theory of society: a theory of society demands the construction of a social model, and all social models, as Max Weber remarks, have something Utopian about them. Conversely, all Utopias are really embodiments of educational theories. We cannot discuss educational theory simply in relation to an existing society, for no educational theory is worth anything unless it can be conceived as transforming that society and, at least to some extent, assimilating it to its own pattern. The moment of leisure, as I have defined it, is that moment which can come only to a fully conscious human being, when he is able to draw back from his activities and compare what he is doing with what he would like to do, or could conceive as better worth doing. This is also the moment at which the sense of a need for education begins, for our words school and scholarship, as Aristotle pointed out, are connected with *schole,* leisure. That is why I spoke of education as something that has for its ultimate goal the vision of an ideal, that is, a theoretically coherent and permanent, social order. In moral terms, we could call this the pattern of the just state.

This leads us to the traditional conception of education that we have inherited from Plato. Plato divides knowledge into two levels: an upper level of theoretical knowledge (theoretical in the sense of *theoria,* vision), which unites itself to permanent ideas or forms, and a lower level of practical knowledge, whose function is to embody these forms or ideas on the level of physical life. What I have referred to in my title as the instruments of mental production consist of the arts, and we may see the major arts in Plato's terms as forming a group of six. Three of these are the arts of *mousike:* music, mathematics, and poetry, and they make up the main body of what Plato means by philosophy, the identifying of the soul of man with the forms or ideas of the world. The other three are the imitative or embodying arts, the arts of *techne,* painting, sculpture, and architecture, which, along with all their satellites and derivatives, unite the body of man with the physical world. In the just state this conception of education is reflected in a hierarchy in which a philosopher-king, supported by guards who have been educated from his point of view, is set in authority over the artisans or producers. Poets who desert their heritage and try to make their art a technical or imitative art have no place in such a state.

The Platonic conception of the relation of education to society is a revolutionary one: the shape of a just society, as education conceives it, is so different from that of society as we know it that the two cannot coexist: one is bound to regard the other as its enemy. When the conception was revived in the Renaissance, it was modified by a more accommodating outlook. Renaissance education still forms a vision of the permanent form of society, and theoretically, the most important person to impart this vision to is the ruler. Society is best off when its king is a philosopher-king, and the ideal of education is the institute of a Christian prince. In this view, however, the education of the prince does not radically alter the existing structure of society: it merely illuminates it. The model here is Xenophon's *Cyropaedia* rather than Plato's *Republic*. But, as is shown in Machiavelli, the actual prince is much more likely to be a man of force and cunning than of wisdom: an incarnation of will, not of reason. Hence in practice the social role of education is more likely to be found in the courtier, the servant and advisor of the prince. The Renaissance had, besides, inherited a medieval tradition in which the most highly educated people were more likely to be clerics than princes, and hence, in the temporal sphere, confined to a similar supporting and advisory role, a civil service rather than a directing power.

The collision between revolutionary and accommodating views of the just state is clearly set out in More's *Utopia,* in a dialogue between More and his friend Hythlodaye, who has been in Utopia. Hythlodaye has returned from Utopia with a Platonic revolutionary view: only the most drastic recasting of Europe into a Utopian mould will do any good to a society in which the "commonwealth" is actually a conspiracy of the rich and powerful. More himself, in the first book, displays a different view: Hythlodaye should, he suggests, come to terms with existing society, at least to the extent of using his Utopian vision in an advisory capacity— informing, modifying, improving and rationalizing the structure of that society, and doing what practically can be done toward assimilating sixteenth-century Europe to a more coherent vision of life. The attitude here is closer to Aristotle's conception of justice than to Plato's, yet included in it is a Christian and Augustinian view that is a logical extension of Plato. If the philosopher-king seeks an identity of his immortal soul with a world of immortal forms, he will eventually have to abdicate as king, as full identity would belong to a contemplative rather than an active life. The ultimate form of the just state can only be embodied in a church or monastic community where the real philosopher-king is God. More's Utopia thus has the same elusive relation to the Christian Church that it has to sixteenth-century Europe. There is a real relation to both, along with an underlying antagonism that goes equally deep.

The Renaissance, then, carried on the traditional conception of education as a vision of the just state, but it had ready at hand a powerful practical method of achieving it. This was humanism, the study, not of an ideal civilization, but of an actual one which, having disappeared, could be studied in its ideal form, as a structure of arts and sciences. This was an educational instrument of a kind foreshadowed by Plato when he went from his vision of the just state in the *Republic* to its sequel, the story of the civilization of Atlantis learned by the Athenians from the older civilization of Egypt. To a considerable extent Roman culture was humanistic in the sense of recreating an earlier Greek culture in its own context, and the Renaissance followed the Romans in recreating a Latinized classical culture in their context. The genuine humanists studied the classics, not as immutable cultural forms in another world, but as informing cultural principles in their world. The classics, in their totality, including Vitruvius on architecture and Columella

on agriculture as well as Virgil and Cicero, made up a coherent structure of knowledge that, properly applied, could
transform Renaissance society into something like its own
pattern of coherence, as the "embers of dead tongues," in
Milton's phrase, kindled a new flame, and the old Roman
Empire became renewed into the Holy Roman Empire, the
temporal power of Christian Europe. At its best, the study of
classical culture promoted a liberalism of outlook that might
otherwise have been impossible in ages so heavily burdened
with religious and political anxieties. The Greek and Roman
cultures could be studied with a genuine detachment, as the
student was committed neither to their religions nor to their
political views and hence was able to separate the ideal or
permanent structure from the historical one.

The humanist conception of education, as late as Arnold
and Newman, still envisaged a roughly Platonic society on
two levels. On the lower level were the producers and artisans, the workers and tradesmen, and those who were concerned with the practical and technical arts. On the upper
level was an aristocracy or leisure class, freed from the
necessity of contributing to social production. The function
of education, on this higher social level, was to transform a
leisure class into a responsible ruling class, trained in the
arts of war and peace, the knowledge both of Plato's guards
and of his philosopher-king. The arts of peace were primarily the musical arts in Plato's sense: they had expanded
into the seven liberal arts in the Middle Ages, but had retained their associations with music, mathematics, and literature. The "music" part of it of course never did have much
to do with what we now think of as music, but was rather a
branch of speculative cosmology. The supremacy of classics
and mathematics, however, was maintained for centuries in
university curricula. These arts represented a permanence

that the technical arts could not match: buildings crumble, even monuments of perennial brass can disappear, but books, while individually expendable, have a unique power of self-perpetuation. Hence a book culture and the study of words and numbers can be used to build and rebuild the permanent forms of society, to establish the sense of continuity that is the genuine control of the social order, statesmanship as distinct from "policy, that heretic," as Shakespeare calls it, which merely swims on the stream of time.

By the nineteenth century, humanist education had to meet the challenge of an entirely new conception of society. This new conception was, once again, clearest in its most revolutionary and Utopian form, as, first, the ideals of the American and more particularly of the French Revolution, and, second, the goals of the socialist revolutionary movement as set out by Marx. This view, like that of Hythlodaye in More, regarded the relation of the upper to the lower level of society as essentially predatory and parasitic. The education that made the ruling class feel responsible was thus primarily a rationalization of their power: it constituted what Marx calls an ideology. In its fully developed form society would be identical with productive society: it would consist entirely of workers and producers. According to Carlyle, who expounded a good deal of this attitude while trying to reverse its movement, the real distinction is not between cultivated leisure and work, but between genuine work, as the expression of the energy and intelligence of man, and the two forms of antiwork that corrupt society. One of these is the idleness, or dandyism as Carlyle calls it, of an unworking aristocracy; the other is drudgery, the menial and degrading results of exploitation and the mechanical division of labor. The distinction between genuine work and drudgery, the subject of a recent study by Hannah Arendt, is developed in

Ruskin and in William Morris: Morris is of particular interest to us here because he thinks of the technical arts as the instruments of social revolution. Architecture and the so-called minor arts, the arts mainly of graphic and pictorial design, are for Morris the forces that transform a society of exploitation into a society of workers and producers.

Faced with this social change, the defenders of humanist education were thrown back, often in spite of themselves, on a conservative view of society, one that emphasizes the permanent values of aristocracy, leisure, cultivation, and of the social conception that Newman calls the "gentleman." Even as late as T. S. Eliot this association of humanism and social conservatism persists. In Arnold there is a remarkable attempt to separate the ideal of leisure and cultivation from the members of the dominant class who normally embody it. The fact that he describes the former as "culture" and the latter as "barbarians" indicates the strength of the effort. Like the humanists of the Renaissance, Arnold gives the primary place to the study of the classics, though only because he thinks of them much as Morris thinks of the arts of design, as the living powers of imagination that transform a class-ridden society into a classless one. But he shows an uneasy awareness of the dwindling number of people who think of the classics in this way, and the growing number of those who either reject them outright as "dead tongues" or accept them mechanically as mere symbols of social status.

In those whose bias was toward science and technology, notably Huxley and Herbert Spencer, we find a liberal view of education halfway between the conservative humanist one and the radical socialist one. Here society is assumed to be primarily a producing society, and the student to be preparing for absorption into a society of producers. Production involves a struggle with nature, and so science, the direct study of nature, comes into the foreground of education. The values of humanistic education, being leisure values, are to be thought of, in a producing society, as spare-time values, not transforming society but refining and ornamenting it. The specific humanist reason for choosing the classics as the basis of literary education thus no longer holds: from this point of view, there are no values in the best Greek and Latin literature that cannot be obtained from the best English literature. Huxley and Spencer were, of course, primarily interested in the new doctrine of evolution, and they thought of evolution as in part a process in which man is constantly being educated by nature. For the most part he is educated reluctantly, involuntarily, and with his mind distracted by his own fantasies, an inattentive and unruly child of Mother Nature. As Huxley says: "The question of compulsory education is settled so far as nature is concerned. Her bill on that question was framed and passed long ago. But, like all compulsory legislation, that of nature is harsh and wasteful in its operation. . . . Nature's discipline is not even a word and a blow, and the blow first; but the blow without the word. It is left to you to find out why your ears are boxed." We see that Huxley's Mother Nature is much like any harassed Victorian mother with a large brood of children, except that she is unusually taciturn: she never scolds, she only whacks. But she is not always a mother: she is a white goddess, and if man accepts her discipline and frames his education on her pattern, he may in time become her lover, even, for brief moments, her master.

From this nineteenth-century view has mainly descended the conception of liberal education as a preparatory period, in which the student is allowed four years to get some perspective on the society around him. After that, in the standard phrase of commencement oratory, he is ready to go out

into the world, conceived as a world of more or less productive activity, where he will use the small percentage of what
he has learned that is relevant to what he is doing, use an
even smaller percentage to help ornament and cultivate his
spare time, and let the rest gradually erode. A decade or so
after graduation one may still have cultivated tastes, but as
a rule one can no longer read the Arabian Nights so fluently in
the original Arabic, or social science textbooks in the original
double Dutch. This conception of education is based on a
Rasselas myth of a youthful prison-paradise, a playpen, as
Robert Hutchins calls it, followed by a descent to the Egypt
of practical life.

It will be seen that this view of liberal education has a
basis that is really antiliberal: a grimly utilitarian standard
is the logical response to it. This standard is modified in
various ways: some things are good in themselves, their own
ends as Newman says, and we have to think of the values of
education as including them too. Or, more obviously, a
knowledge of the more permanent principles of the arts and
sciences turns out to be more practically useful than the kind
of technical training that becomes obsolete as soon as one
has learned it. But as long as we accept, even unconsciously,
a vision of society in which the machinery of production
assumes an overwhelming and inescapable urgency, our defenses of the liberal arts and sciences will continue to have a
panic-stricken tone. There is residual panic even in the
question of what knowledge is most worthwhile, for in the
time-word "while" lurks the thought "so little time," with its
suggestion that a pathetically small part of one's life is spent in
acquiring knowledge. The conception of society as consisting
functionally only of workers and producers was one of the
great nineteenth-century contributions to thought. But con-

sidering that it has become a stock response to say that the main problem of the twentieth century is the problem of leisure, surely we need to develop a view of education that incorporates this problem. The natural drive of the producing society is not democratic but oligarchic or managerial: it increases inequalities of privilege instead of reducing them, and in itself is no longer capable of leading us to the vision of the just state.

Today, the machinery of production appears to be steadily declining in the proportion of time and attention that it requires. I am not speaking of automation, which is not a cause but an effect of this process: I mean simply that the proportion of work to leisure which according to the Book of Genesis was established by God himself on a ratio of six to one is rapidly changing in the direction of a ratio of one to one. This makes for a social situation in which dull, meaningless, and exploited labor is less inevitable, and hence idleness and distraction are less inevitable as reactions against it. We are accustomed to thinking that everyone needs to be functionally related to his society through the work he does. But if leisure comes to occupy so much of so many people's lives, the question of finding a social function in leisure becomes increasingly important. This is already a problem of some urgency with women, as middle-class housewives are the obvious victims of a machinery of production so overefficient that it can only continue to operate by turning as many people as possible into full-time consumers. We appear, then, to be entering a period in which work and leisure are not embodied in different classes, but should be thought of as two aspects, nearly equal in importance, of the same life. Every citizen may be not only a Martha, troubled about many things, but a Mary who has chosen the better part, and the question "What does he know?" becomes as relevant to defining one's social function as the question "What does he do?"

The vast network of educational and cultural activities, which includes schools, universities, churches, theaters, concerts, art galleries and museums, adult education programs, and many other things, such as recreational and physical education, which I cannot deal with here, is thus gradually taking shape as the *other half* of society. Some countries, including Canada, have a nationalized program of television, radio, and films, which is, or is supposed to be, more educational in its aims than the so-called private media that are conscripts in the army of production. One would hope to see an increasingly large proportion of such media desert advertising for education, or, at least, become more concerned to guide than merely to reflect public taste. One would hope to see the present notion disappear that mass media must be controlled either by propaganda or by advertising, that the former means totalitarianism and slavery and the latter democracy and freedom. The confusion of the liberal and the laissez faire is still very much with us. One would hope to see the machinery of production operated with less hysteria through the gradual elimination of superfluous goods, including the waste products of war. These are Utopian hopes, but without Utopian hopes there can be no clear vision of social reality. In such a society it would be appropriate that universities should no longer be almost wholly concerned, as teaching institutions, with young people in the few lucid intervals that occur during four years of the mating season, but would make a place also for adults who could keep dropping into the university at various periods of their lives as an intellectual retreat.

In this social context, the question of what knowledge is

worthwhile would not have the implication that knowledge is obtained mainly during a period of preparing for life. Life will not stay around to be prepared for, nor, in a world where the coding, housing, and retrieving of information is itself one of the biggest activities there is, can life be conceived as anything apart from a continuous learning process. The essential aim of all early education should be the inculcating of a lifetime habit. This takes me back to my original remark that for a genuine student the knowledge of most worth is the subject to which he has already committed himself. One would normally expect that the subject which forms a student's "major" would be the basis of a permanent interest in that subject. It is one function of general education, I should think, to establish a context for special cultural interests. Every field of knowledge is the center of all knowledge, and general education should help the student to see how this is true for his chosen field.

It is obvious, as was also said at the beginning, that a cultivated and well-informed interest in a subject is something different from scholarship, with its dependence on research libraries and laboratories. As the somewhat sinister phrase "productive scholar" indicates, scholarship is part of the army of production: the scholar is not necessarily, *qua* scholar, an educated man at all, and he works in an area where the division of labor is at its most thoroughgoing. The editor of Shakespeare and the chemist live in different scholarly worlds, and proposals to make the humanist memorize the second law of thermodynamics and the scientist a speech from *Macbeth* will not bring them together. What brings them together is social, not intellectual, the fact that they are both citizens of their society with a common stake in that society. The only knowledge that is worthwhile is the knowledge that leads to wisdom, for knowledge without wisdom is a body without life. But no form of knowledge necessarily does or cannot do that: the completing of the structure has something to do with one's sense of the place of knowledge in the total human situation, ideal as well as actual.

Because we have tended to think of leisure as occasional or preparatory, and leisure-time activities as merely filling up the cracks of a busy life, the creative arts, which are particularly the symbols of cultivation, have never reached their true educational proportions. I think that what is true of scholarship is also true of the creative arts: those who paint and write and compose are, again, producers. The process of liberal education seems to me to be concerned more with understanding and responding to the arts than with producing them, though of course this is a matter of emphasis, not of definition. As Castiglione showed for the Renaissance courtier, the artist needs to be complemented by the cultivated amateur, who represents the social vision of an educated public that has some idea what to do with the artist's work. Hence education in the arts is primarily critical: it struggles to attain a conscious knowledge and understanding of a kind that is normally detached from the creative process itself, though it should be as useful to the creative artist as to anyone else. The chief deficiency in today's literature, for example, is not the lack of good writers, but the lack of a reading public sufficiently large, informed, and articulate to establish the real social importance of the good writer.

The importance of the creative arts becomes obvious in proportion as social leisure increases: they are the primary elements of the cultivated life and of all social ideals. But their importance does not stop here: they are also, in the phrase of my title, the primary instruments of mental production. We have seen that two arts, literature and mathematics, held a leading place in Platonic, medieval, and humanistic conceptions of education, and their place today is as central as ever, although the classical literatures are now reinforced by the modern ones. The contemporary reason for their importance is that the arts of words and numbers are not only arts in themselves but informing languages for other disciplines. Words inform the bodies of knowledge that we call the humanities, as well as most of the social sciences; mathematics informs the sciences, more particularly the physical sciences. I suppose the scientific part of general education would be general science, and it is always something of a tour de force to make science accessible and profitable to the unspecializing student. But of course the more the student understands of the language of mathematics, the less difficult the tour de force has to be. I think that literature, the art of words, has a similar relation to the other verbal disciplines, and that the shape of the arguments of the controversial subjects, religion, philosophy, political theory, is ultimately a poetic shape.

Education is concerned with two worlds: the world that man lives in and the world he wants to live in. It would, of course, be nonsense to say that the former was the business of the sciences and the latter the business of the humanities and the arts. But it is true that science is primarily the study of the order of nature, the world that is there: it is true also that the form of the world man wants to live in is revealed by the form of the world he keeps trying to build, the world of cities and gardens and libraries and highways that is a world of art. We come closer to their relation if we say that the two great divisions of liberal knowledge embody two moral attitudes which are also intellectual virtues. The distinctive intellectual virtue of science is detachment, the objective consideration of evidence, the drawing of rational conclusions from evidence, the rejection of all devices for cooking or manipulating the evidence. Such a virtue is most obvious in the sciences that are founded on the repeatable experiment. But even in fields that are non-experimental and non-predictive, such as history, the scholar needs the same kind of detachment and is bound by the same code of honor to the extent that the nature of his subject permits. Only in the creative arts, perhaps, is one free of the scientific code, and only there because detachment is replaced by a kind of craftsmanship that is psychologically very similar.

But in the arts, particularly the literary arts, we become aware of many human factors relevant to them but not to science as such: emotion, value, aesthetic standards, the portrayal of objects of desire and hope and dream as realities, the explicit preference of life to death, of growth to petrifaction, of freedom to enslavement. Literature is not detached but concerned: it deals with what is there in terms of what man wants and does not want. The same sense of the relevance of concern enters into many other verbal areas, into religion (where the concern is "ultimate," in Tillich's phrase), and a great deal of philosophy and history and political theory and psychology. It extends into most areas of applied science, and if it does not enter pure science as such, that is only because the detachment of science is the aspect of concern that is appropriate to science. And just as the language of science seems to be largely mathematical, so the language of concern is verbal, but verbal in a certain way. Briefly, the language of concern is the language of myth. Myth is the structural principle of literature that enters into and gives form to the verbal disciplines where concern is relevant. Man's views of the world he wants to live in, of the world he does not want to live in, of his situation and destiny and heritage, of the world he is trying to make and of the world that resists his efforts forms in every age a huge mythological structure, and the subjects I have just listed form the main elements of it. I call it a structure, and, sometimes, as in the Middle Ages, it really does seem to be one, the extent to which the Middle Ages unified its mythology being a source of great admiration to later times. In our own day we are more aware of variety and disagreement in our mythology, but the connecting links are there, and it is a part of the task of general education to try to expose them.

Many of those who are engaged in building up this mythopoeic structure—poets, theologians, philosophers, cultural historians—keep eagerly scanning the physical sciences for formulae that they can annex, thereby showing that scientific evidence confirms their world-picture. In the eighteenth century there was great religious, philosophical, and poetic excitement over the world-view that Newton had developed, though on analysis it was not so much his actual science that caused the excitement as the fact that Newton, who himself had speculative interests, had thrown out such suggestions as that space was the sensorium of deity, in addition to framing his laws of motion and gravitation. Evolution, similarly, set off a great wave of mythopoeic speculation ranging from Bernard Shaw's creative will to theories about society that had much more to do with Malthus than with Darwin. Various conceptions borrowed from Einstein, Planck, and Heisenberg have been used to decorate more recent world-pictures, and the law of entropy, taken out of its thermodynamic context and applied to the entire universe, gives us a cosmology sufficiently pointless and lugubrious to sound very modern in this existential age.

These examples are somewhat discouraging: they all seem to me to be phony, and I doubt if any of them would be regarded, in the sciences that suggested them, as founded on a genuine and well-proportioned knowledge of those sciences. I would even risk the suggestion that the physical sciences have never contributed anything to the mythopoeic world-picture except through misunderstanding and misapplication. If that is true, then the moral is clearly that science is its own world-view, and should be distinguished from the mythical one, even though it may be another mythology. Any cultivated person can become acquainted with both without trying to reconcile them, and without suffering from schizophrenia through failing to do so. Doubtless the world we see and the world we create meet somewhere at some point of identity, but keeping the two eyes of knowledge focussed on that point seems better than a Cyclopean single vision. It is particularly in the religious area of the mythical vision that this is true. There is a natural impetus of religion toward idolatry: the instinct that created gods out of nature in primitive life still keeps trying to project God from human concerns into the order of nature. The God of nature is dead, because he was never alive, but the fact that there is no time and no place for God in the scientific world-view does not refute the religious aspect of the mythical one.

I am not, of course, speaking of philosophical efforts to co-ordinate scientific world-views in themselves, which form a different kind of activity. And what I am attacking, in any case, is not the integrating of myth and science, if it can be done, but the forcible conversion of science to myth. I spoke of detachment and concern as the virtues of the two attitudes, but for each virtue there is a corresponding vice. The vice of detachment is indifference: the feeling that one's immediate concern is separable from the total human concern—that a man can be an island entire of himself. The indifferent man, in science or business or whatever, does what seems useful to himself at the moment, and shrugs off irritably the suggestion that it might be harmful to society, or even to his own better self. The trouble with indifference is that it cannot remain indifference. The only forms of human reality are life and death, and if the hopes and dreams and desires and values of humanity which are essential to life are rejected, life itself is rejected. Sooner or later indifference must be conscripted by aggression, and find its fulfilment in war, in the promotion of death on a total scale.

The vice of concern, on the other hand, is anxiety. We have anxiety when a society seizes on one myth and attempts to pound the whole of knowledge and truth into a structure conforming to it. The simplest statement of this kind of anxiety is the remark attributed to the Caliph Omar, when about to burn the Alexandrian Library, that all the books in it either agreed or disagreed with the Koran, and were therefore either superfluous or blasphemous. Similar anxieties dominated Christian Europe for centuries, and provided more than enough evidence that the desire to persecute was an essential part of them. Marxism forms the same kind of anxiety-myth today, and it too has its Omars demonstrating that all forms of knowledge are either consistent with it or wrong. Hysterical anxiety-groups on the extreme right in American life also work in the direction of setting up a myth of "Americanism" as the criterion for all statements of fact or opinion. It is generally felt that such groups exert a subversive influence on American culture that is out of all proportion to their numbers, to say nothing of their intelligence. If so, then something is lacking in the educational resources of the saner part of the country.

To sum up: the instruments of mental production are the creative arts and the bodies of knowledge they inform. These bodies make up two larger bodies, mythology and science, man's view of his own destiny and his view of the world around him. These larger bodies are distinguishable, but not separate, and the moral attitudes that make them possible, concern and detachment, interpenetrate in all knowledge. Mythology in particular, on the level of general education, forms an initiatory pattern of education: understanding the traditional lore of one's society. The basis of it is social mythology, the clichés and stock responses that pour into the mind from conversation and the mass media, including school textbooks. The purpose of social mythology is to create the adjusted, that is, the docile and obedient citizen, and it occupies an overwhelming proportion of American elementary education. I think this is the source of the deficiency I have just noted: the myth of the American way of life does not distinguish the reality from the rationalized facade of that life. Above social mythology is the mythical structure formed by the humanities and the vision of nature afforded by general science, the purpose of which is to create the informed and participating citizen. Above this is the world of art and scholarship, which is to be left to shape itself, and acknowledged to have the authority to reshape the structure of general education below it at any time. Where an initiatory mythology controls the whole structure of education, as it did in medieval Europe and does now in Communist China, tolerance is a negative virtue, a matter of deciding how much deviation is consistent with the safety of the myth. Where art and scholarship are autonomous, tolerance is a positive and creative force, the unity of detachment and concern.

When I say that education is the study of society in its stable and permanent form, I do not, naturally, mean an unchanging form. I mean that genuine society preserves the continuity of the dead, the living and the unborn, the memory of the past, the reality of the present, and the anticipation of the future which is the one unbreakable social contract. Continuity and consistency are the only sources of human dignity and they cannot be attained in the dissolving phantasmagoria of the newspaper world, where we have constantly to focus on an immediate crisis, where a long-term memory is almost a handicap. The term "liberal" applied to education, again, reminds us that there is not necessarily any principle of freedom in political democracy, in economic laissez faire, or in the separation of state and church. All these may be signs of a measure of freedom in society, but they are not sources of it. There can be no freedom except in the power to realize the possibilities of human life, both in oneself and for others, and the basis of that power is the continuing vision of a continuing city.

A TRANSATLANTIC VIEW OF
"WHAT KNOWLEDGE IS
WORTH HAVING"

Sir John Cockcroft

I have been invited to give a transatlantic view of what knowledge is worth having. This view is inevitably biased by my own early interest in nuclear physics, and later in nuclear technology, and by my more general interests as they have developed throughout my life.

For several thousand years thinkers and philosophers have been interested in the origin and development of the universe, and we are, and should be, no less interested today, though our ideas have greatly changed from the ideas of the writers of Genesis. Today our ideas are still changing with the continuing discoveries of optical and radio astronomy. For some time there have been two rival theories about the origin and development of the universe. The so-called "big bang" theory assumes that at $T=0$, about ten billion years ago, some unknown event resulted in the appearance of matter in the form of hydrogen or neutrons and that the universe evolved from this matter. The rival theory assumes that matter in the form of hydrogen is being continuously created and that the universe is in an approximately "steady state." This theory is now losing ground in the face of experimental evidence. The course of evolution after the initial appearance of matter was and is determined by the four basic forces of the universe—the gravitational field, the electromagnetic forces between electrically charged particles, and the nuclear forces that become dominant when nuclear particles, protons, and neutrons are close together. The gravitational forces between the primeval particles results in their drawing together in clusters to form galaxies, and within galaxies, stars. As the process goes on the stars are heated up by the release of gravitational energy to central temperatures of several million degrees. So by this time the hydrogen nuclei begin to make sufficiently energetic collisions for the nuclear forces to come into play, and this results in the fusion of protons to form helium, resulting in the release of nuclear energy. This in turn produces a further increase in the central temperature of the evolving stars. From then on heavier and heavier elements are progressively synthesized in the nuclear furnace. In some stars the course of evolution results finally in a very violent nuclear explosion spewing out a whole gamut of elements into space to be brought together again in the course of time and formed into new stars. An event of this kind was observed by Korean astronomers in 1054, and the debris of the explosion is today the supernova known as the Crab Nebula, which still emits light and radio waves.

During the last three years astronomers have observed even more interesting and exciting objects, amongst them the so-called Quasars, objects which emit radio and light waves with some of the characteristics of stars, but emitting far more energy than whole galaxies. So much so that even nuclear energy cannot account for its magnitude. Some of these objects at the boundaries of the known universe move away from us with almost the velocity of light. Other objects found by balloon flights emit X-rays and little visible light. They may be the final state of a dying star, with as much material as is contained in our sun compressed into a space only ten miles or so in diameter. Such stars might have central temperatures several hundred times that of the center of our sun and a surface temperature of millions of degrees. So there are "more things in heaven and earth than are dreamt of in our philosophy."

This fascinating world of the almost infinitely large is connected with the world of the almost infinitely small, for, during the evolution of stars and in the more violent cosmic events, the inhabitants of a subnuclear underworld play an important role. This subnuclear world consists of the transient members, such as neutrinos, mesons, hyperons, antimatter, which are born in violent nuclear collisions; these change thereafter from one member of the species into another, and after a sequence of changes appear as known stable particles, such as electrons. These objects have an order of their own; they can be grouped into families whose underlying significance is still obscure. They are certainly connected with the four basic forces of the universe. The reason why nuclear physicists wish to build ever more powerful nuclear accelerators is because of the great fundamental importance of these studies.

As earthbound inquirers, we should take a particular interest in how and when our planet was born and how life developed here. We now believe that the earth was formed from cold aggregates of dust and gases associated with the early development of the sun about five billion years ago. I must admit, however, that estimates of the age of the earth have been steadily increasing since Bishop Ussher's seventeenth-century estimate of six thousand years and Lord Kelvin's nineteenth-century estimate of about one hundred million years. Rutherford once gave a lecture to an audience including Lord Kelvin in which he was preparing to state how the heat liberated by radium had increased the estimates of the age of the earth and thus vitiated the forecast of Lord Kelvin. To his relief Lord Kelvin fell fast asleep, but as Rutherford came to the important point, he said, "I saw the old bird sit up, open an eye, and cock a baleful glance at me. Then a sudden inspiration came, and I said 'Lord Kelvin had limited the age of the earth provided no *new* source of energy was discovered. This prophetic utterance refers to what we are now considering tonight—Radium.' Behold! the old boy beamed upon me."

Our ideas on the origin of life have also changed a great deal since the poetic concept of the Garden of Eden and have developed rapidly during the last decade. George Wald told, at the centenary celebrations of the National Academy of Sciences three years ago, that rocks in southern Ontario, estimated to be 1.6 billion years old, contain evidence of micro-organisms including fungi and algae. Therefore complex molecules allowing photosynthesis to take place must have evolved by that time. Professor Calvin told us in a recent Bakerian lecture to the Royal Society of London that the rocks two and one-half billion years old contain organic molecules closely related to the green pigments of plants, so that the synthesis of complex molecules, such as those important molecular building blocks—the amino acids— must have taken place from the earth's initial atmosphere of hydrogen, water, ammonia, and methane within about two billion years. It is now possible by laboratory experiments to show how this evolution could occur in the early atmosphere aided by radiation from thunderstorms and by solar ultraviolet radiation. The evolution of complex molecules having the power to reproduce themselves must have developed in the oceans, leading to the final semimiracle of the double-stranded helical molecule DNA and its associated molecule RNA. DNA, the central molecule of the biological world, is just as important as the atomic nucleus in the physical world. One can think of it as behaving like a magnetic tape, storing through the sequence of four kinds of molecular units the information required for the fabrication of the ten thousand or so kinds of proteins and enzymes that control the chemical factory of human bodies. It stores the information that determines whether we have black skins or white skins, blue eyes or grey eyes, mathematical ability or the lack of it. The characteristics of a virus are determined by the sequence of about five thousand of the four basic molecular units. The full set of characteristics of man require several billion units to spell it out, and so there is room for infinite diversity in human beings. Even provision for evolution is built into this remarkable molecule, for the omission or interchange of one of the four basic units can result in a mutation, usually harmful, but in the past helpful in evolutionary development of organisms.

An appreciation of the way life has evolved is of special importance in the future world, since biologists think they are on the verge of fabricating simple forms of life from the basic building blocks, using at first biological templates. Through the growing knowledge of the central control mechanism, they may in time find the cure for diseases such as cancer. In the long run they may even be able to cure inborn genetic damage. Biology today is being taught more and more on an interdisciplinary basis, starting with the processes in the living cell and the integration of these processes into the lives of organisms. A knowledge of modern developments in biology is certainly worth having.

The physical sciences are also tending to group themselves for teaching and research on an interdisciplinary basis. Materials science has become more and more exciting and important, as its theoretical basis becomes firmer with the application of the quantum theory of solids and the development of important new techniques, such as the electron and field ion microscopes, which have allowed us to see the structure of solids down to the atomic level. These advances have led to the great range of solid-state electronic devices, such as transistors, solar cells, infrared detectors, solid-state rectifiers, and masers and lasers, some of which have had great technological applications. The increased knowledge has also greatly improved our control of the properties of metals, ceramics, and plastics, and has made possible new developments in many fields, such as jet engines, space flight, nuclear power, and buildings.

The earth sciences embrace the structure and physics of the earth and its environment. The physics of the earth has great practical importance in a civilization that now relies for a large part of its energy on oil and natural gas, and in Britain today we watch with great interest the explorations guided by the geophysicists for oil and natural gas under the North Sea, hoping that we will be as fortunate as Holland in finding large reservoirs of natural gas which can be fed into our industries and homes. Advances in the earth sciences have made possible the detection of earthquakes and nuclear explosions at ranges of up to 10,000 kilometers, and re-markable advances have been made through arrays of seismographs and the application of modern information theory, so that, if the political barrier can be overcome, I still have hope that a complete test-ban treaty can be achieved. The science of meteorology has been greatly helped by the advent of powerful electronic computers and better input information from satellites and weather stations, so that short-range forecasting is becoming much more reliable and even long-range forecasts are becoming interesting. Attempts to control rainfall and to divert hurricanes are still a challenge for the future.

The basic disciplines of physics—dynamics, electricity and magnetism, waves and oscillations, quantum physics—underlie the whole of modern science and continue to be worth knowing, and they are now being taught in a more enlightened way, conveying more of the spirit and method of science and certainly much more of the physics of the twentieth century than they did a few years ago.

I will not attempt to speak in any detail about the work of the chemists and their tremendous fertility in synthesizing new molecules, new pharmaceuticals, new pesticides, new herbicides, which are so important in industry, medicine, and agriculture. They still have many new worlds to conquer, especially in biochemistry, resulting in part from the interdisciplinary attack on their problems.

I need hardly say that mathematics is worth knowing, not only for its own sake, but because it underlies the whole of the biological and physical sciences and is now an indispensable tool for the social sciences.

Technology does not normally form part of a liberal arts education, though there are arguments that, by not providing outlets for creative work in early education, we suppress many of the innate technological abilities of many students. It is important to appreciate how new technology develops from creative science and how developments in technology are likely to affect the world during the remainder of this century—during a good part of your working lives.

Today the process of technological change is accelerating rather than diminishing. For energy and electricity we will rely increasingly on oil and natural gas and the new fuel, nuclear energy. After working in the 1930's on the transmutation of atomic nuclei by bombardment with artificially accelerated protons, I have been fortunate in being able to work during the last twenty years on the application of the energy stored in atomic nuclei to the production of electricity on a large scale. Nuclear power stations having an output of over a million kilowatts are now being built in Britain and in this country, which will produce electricity at about 10 per cent below the cost of electricity from the most modern coal and oil power stations on the same sites. So the threshold of competitive nuclear power has been passed, and by 1980 between a quarter and a half of British electricity production will come from nuclear power stations. A not unimportant advantage is that future power stations will not belch forth millions of tons a year of SO_2 and dirt into the atmosphere to foul our lungs and cities.

During the last twenty years we have seen piston-engine aircraft replaced by turbo props, and in turn by turbo jets, and now our aircraft manufacturers are working on the next generation of supersonic aircraft, so that in the 1970's we shall be able to cross the Atlantic in less time than that required to travel to and from the airports and to pass through New York Customs. My friends working in the aerospace industry in California assure you that we will be able to travel between any two points of the globe by rocket before the end of the century, but I am glad that this will be too late for me.

World communications will become easier and more rapid through submarine cables carrying thousands of simultaneous telephone conversations, and cables will be supplemented by satellites. Through international TV it is possible to watch and hear the great symphony orchestras of the world, the Bolshoi Ballet, our leading artists, sportsmen, and politicians. Data important for governments, business, and research workers will be transmitted from country to country through this network of communications and stored in the capacious memories of powerful computers, to be extracted from them by those who possess the necessary code—by government departments, banks, industries, scholars, and scientists. There is already a giant central computer for airline bookings in this country; the United States Internal Revenue is installing one, no doubt to record and calculate income tax liabilities with increasing efficiency. Our factories will be greatly affected by this revolution. Skilled operators of machine tools are already being partially replaced by programmed machine tools, and the operators are being elevated to programmers, punching tape to control the operations, thereby enabling much more complex and accurate work to be carried out. Whole factories, such as steel mills, and worldwide businesses, such as oil, are beginning to be centrally controlled by computers. Many of these developments will take a great deal of the remaining drudgery out of industry and will require a higher degree of training in an increasing proportion of our people. I do not think we are heading for a world of robots. These developments will certainly provide more leisure time as the official working week continues to shorten. All the more reason for a broad liberal arts education to prepare for the use of increasing amounts of leisure.

The study of the social sciences is becoming increasingly popular in universities. Indeed the development of technology and industry requires an increasing participation of economists and sociologists. There is certainly far more to be gained by sociological innovation in British industry, and perhaps even in some sections of American industry, by sweeping away the restrictions of the past than from new developments of technology.

In spite of the Keynesian revolution and the importation of university economists into government, our economies still seem to be managed in an empirical stop-go manner. The applied economists of the University of Cambridge are experimenting with computer models of the economy, which they hope will enable them to give a quantitative picture of the economy in 1970 and the requirements to enable a 4 per cent or so growth rate to be achieved without running into recurrent balance of payment difficulties. Economics must certainly be kept on the list of subjects worth knowing.

The development of large-scale technological projects will confront us with important economic and social choices. What, for example, are the social and economic advantages of a supersonic aircraft project costing several billion dollars as against subsonic flight? What are the relative advantages of different transport systems? Can we reduce the choking up of our cities with commuters' cars by providing more and better high-speed public transportation? How can we best rebuild our cities, our road and rail systems, to take account of the tremendously rapid increase of the car and truck population that shows little signs of diminishing? What are the economic and social benefits of the space-travel programs of the United States and Russia? Apart from the technological spin-off, such as micro-electronics and microcomputers, what do we gain from explorations in space? There is certainly great scientific interest in determining whether primitive forms of life exist on Mars, but we will find no Martians. So the astronauts will have to travel to other stellar systems to find evidence of human-like life. George Wald of Harvard has estimated that there may be 10^{17} planets suitable for life in the already observed universe. But to travel to the nearest star, α Centauri, would take the astronauts a lifetime with present rocket speeds, and four years if they could travel the speed of light—but no doubt our rocket technologists are already thinking of nuclear propelled rockets to enable them to achieve their ambitions. How much of our resources are we willing to spend on this?

The study of the history of civilization must continue to be part of a liberal education, not only for its intrinsic interest, but for its importance in appreciating present and future developments. I have always been fascinated by the broad sweep of the development, starting with Sumeria, Egypt, and the Middle Eastern civilizations, as revealed by the labors of the archaeologists and the manuscripts and monuments of the past. Students in Britain can take delight in the legacies of past ages, the great earthworks, castles, and dykes of prehistoric times, the Roman roads, Hadrian's wall built to keep out the Scots, the once luxurious villas with central heating systems scattered in pleasant places about England. We have a great legacy of cathedrals, ruined abbeys, village churches, castles— most of them works of art. These legacies are matched in many other parts of the world, particularly in Europe, Asia, the jungles of Yucatan, and the buried cities of South America.

A study of the origins of modern science should be part of these historical studies, starting with the Greeks and thence to the work of the early astronomers and so to Galileo and Newton's great synthesis of the laws of gravitation and dynamics.

A study of history should surely include the study of politics—the forces which influence vital decisions in the modern world. I have been reading Arthur Schlesinger's *A Thousand Days* (Boston: Houghton Mifflin, 1965), which gives a first-hand account of the forces, the multiplicity of advisors, and the pressure groups that influence top-level decisions, such as the "Bay of Pigs" expedition, the second Cuban crisis, disarmament negotiations, and the Southeast Asian wars. Nowhere else have I read such an intimate account of the conflicting information and advice that faces a head of state in making his often agonizing decisions. Even scientists are revealed as offering conflicting and often dubious advice.

I think you should have a general knowledge of the

problems of the so-called developing countries, and the efforts through your AID program and our Ministry of Overseas Development to improve their economies and standards of living. The Americans, as well as the British, have long been active in the educational field in the developing countries, but our efforts and help have been too small in scale, so that Nigeria, for example, was left after independence with only one doctor for each thirty thousand of the population—most of them being in cities—and only about five hundred indigenous scientists and engineers. So it is not surprising that 40 per cent of the children die before the age of five. The Peace Corps and the British Voluntary Service Overseas program provide an opportunity of learning about aid at first hand.

We must become aware, in particular, of the tremendous importance of reducing the rate of growth of population in many parts of the world, such as India and Latin America, where population growth almost counterbalances any benefits received from economic aid. Biological research today is providing new methods of reducing population growth. We must devote more effort to applying the new knowledge by channeling more of our aid into this work and by helping to combat the political inertia and theological dogma that hold up a solution or mitigation of this very urgent problem.

In a liberal education you should, of course, be continually exposed to the influence of literature, the visual arts, and music, if only because they form an essential part of a good life.

The teaching of English and literature is changing, though not so fast as the teaching of science. In the 1880's, the teaching of literature moved into the vacuum left by the decay of academic theology. Matthew Arnold and others asked that literature be allowed to take over the tasks of moral enrichment and training formerly assigned to religious teaching. It was confidently felt that a man reading Shakespeare or Keats under academic guidance would be a finer, more humane, more balanced human being.

At the same time, the tremendous upsurge of German critical scholarship suggested that modern languages could be studied with the same rigor as Hebrew and Greek and Latin. There were countless English literary texts to edit, to explain, to analyze historically and philologically. There were glossaries and concordances to compile, and so forth.

Today neither of these two fundamental points is entirely or demonstrably relevant. For all too obvious reasons we are no longer at all confident that a literary, humanistic education does very much to make men better or incapable of political stupidity, social confusion, or personal vileness. At the same time, we are obviously running out of texts to edit and really major historical problems to clear up. What remains—as in the classics—are the minutiae and the pedantries.

In place of this teaching of the past, my literary friends in Cambridge tell me that there is a growth of interest in comparative literature. A tremendous impetus—comparable to that which archaeology and anthropology gave to theology—will result from the use of comparative methods in the study of European and Anglo-American literature. A man whose essential academic training is limited to his own vernacular and to one tradition is not, I think, very usefully educated.

A closer association between literary studies and history and sociology should prove very stimulating. Literature and art do not exist in isolation from the social, economic, and political contexts and mythologies of their time; studied in that context they take on meanings and effects that cannot be separated from their formal structures.

Some of you will attend formal courses in music and art. No doubt you also arrange your own concerts and plays as English students do in Churchill College. Modern colleges should be adorned with the art of the present as well as the art of the past. Churchill College collects, through gifts, the works of our highly talented young silversmiths, drawings and paintings of our contemporaries, modern sculpture—including a Barbara Hepworth, and soon, we hope, a more curvilinear Henry Moore. We have a modern French tapestry by Lurçat, which adorns our undergraduate library; we have two paintings by Sir Winston Churchill and a fine portrait of him by Orpen, together with rubbings from the temple friezes of Angkor Wat and English churches. We are catholic in our tastes.

You may think that this account of what I think is worth knowing is all very interesting, but how can such a wide-ranging collection be translated into a "required core." I don't think that it is possible to compress everything that is worth knowing into a "required core," or indeed into a three-year course. On the contrary, learning and knowing should be a continuous process through life. In later university years, especially in graduate student years, it is necessary to specialize. But with increasing age our interests inevitably broaden. Life is all too short to explore all the fascinating avenues that open. A well-known poet said in his inaugural lecture at Cambridge: "The pleasure of learning and knowing, though not the keenest, is yet the least perishable of pleasures; the least subject to external things and the play of chance and the wear of time. And as a prudent man puts money by to serve as a provision for the material wants of his old age, so too he needs to lay up against the end of his days provision for the intellect."

UNDERGRADUATES AND THE
SCIENTIFIC ENTERPRISE

J. A. Simpson

It has been my misfortune not to be present at the discussions of this conference. Consequently, as we draw toward the end of this week of debate, reassessment, and refreshment of goals within the college, I am curious to know whether there is a clarification of what are for me two of the most worrisome and critical questions facing our undergraduate program. Briefly they are, first—How do students whose life interests center on scholarship and action outside the sciences grasp the beauty, breadth, and impact of science on their lives and their society? And second—How do we stimulate and sustain the creative urge in the potential scientists within our college student body? My main discussion will focus on the second question, not only because I believe it is one that I may attack more definitively, but also because it is the simpler problem. In addition, if we cannot resolve the second question we shall certainly not answer the first. I have no unique solutions to offer and only tentative thoughts on what may be the right direction to take, so let us begin.

First, let me reformulate the second question. It might read as follows: When, and under what circumstances, are students to be given the opportunity to participate in the real work of scholarly pursuit and scientific research with the objective of finding out whether their zest for knowledge is matched by their dedication to face the discipline, hardships, and failures leading to the emergence of original contributions and the demonstration of creative ability? Shall this challenge be made in the college, or is it, as often thought, only practical for the graduate school? Should it be part of our assessment of your four years at Chicago? I am certain that related questions have already been phrased in more eloquent terms at this conference and are intimately related to the existing and proposed honors programs in the college. But the solution of the problem has a qualitatively different character than the conventional honors program, and I hope that this distinction becomes clear from my discussion. Some university faculty have made efforts over the past years informally to recognize this issue and offer opportunities to students on a limited basis. There have been several successful efforts at an informal level, and I shall refer to them later.

High on the list of factors which motivated your choice of Chicago is the human aspiration for understanding and contributing to science, or society, through scholarly pursuits and scientific inquiry. For many of you at some time during your college years, however, there develops a dichotomy of purpose and a sense of frustration. On the one hand, formal education and scheduled classes provide major sequences of study designed to place you successfully in competition with others entering graduate schools anywhere in the nation, or in the world. This we do well with increasing confidence. But on the other hand, there dwells the uneasy, underlying desire for expressing one's own talents, mixed and undisciplined as they may be, to find out if we have "got what it takes" for commitment to a life of science or scholarly pursuit as it exists outside the classroom. In my opinion it is not reasonable to postpone this confrontation to the years of graduate training. Many of you have been cheated out of an adequate education in high school and are now "on the move" to make up for lost time. Most of you are in the age group somewhere between eighteen and twenty-three. The history of our civilization confirms that these are the years when most talented individuals begin to emerge in the arts, sciences, and humanities.

Although my remarks apply to the humanities and social sciences, as well as mathematics and the natural sciences, I emphasize the sciences because it is here that the principal difficulties appear to rest at present in the modern college, and the issues—at least for me—are most sharply defined. Later I shall try to consider the relevance of these matters to the college in general. To restate the problem, we are seeking ways to provide opportunities for some qualified students to participate in ongoing scientific research instead of arranging to meet the students on the neutral ground of the classroom, or the prepared honors essay. It is the involvement in some aspect of the research of the moment that so frequently fires up a young man or woman, casting their formal studies in a new light. It is within this framework that the student recognizes the beauty of unfolding the secrets of nature and discovers his kinship—at least in spirit—to the artist. The student also discovers in this framework that it is a mixture of many personal qualities which leads to success in the sciences. Intelligence is essential, but not the overriding condition. Personal drive, dedication, and curiosity play equally important roles. These characteristics may be regrouped as imagination, curiosity, invention, and action. They are combined in various ways, in various mixtures, and rarely are all of them combined in one person. I remember some years ago Robert Oppenheimer summing it up in the following words: "One of the charms of the scientific enterprise is how deficient we can be in many of these qualities and still play some meaningful part in it." Each of us strives to contribute. Even if it is only a small discovery, the excitement and satisfaction to the individual—and the contribution to science—are irreversible.

It is our unshaken belief, on the basis of the development of science and scientists over the last century, that the drive and curiosity which motivate senior investigators within the university also provide the best intellectual environment for students to learn and to be inspired by participation in scientific discovery—no matter how small that participation may be. Indeed, the two components, research and the metamorphosis of students into scientists, catalyze each other so that the result is a higher level of excellence than is normally achieved by the pursuit of either component alone. These activities are most fruitfully conducted within the walls of the university research laboratory. Our college within a modern university is in a unique position to bring students into contact with original research. Chicago is especially fortunate since it is a leader in the main areas of scientific inquiry and working on many of the frontiers of knowledge.

What are the means for coupling the students into the scientific enterprise on campus? To understand the possibilities and limitations it is essential to understand some of the characteristics of present-day science and how it differs from the science of fifty or even thirty years ago. It is the story of the emergence of the scientific enterprise. The progress of science is dependent on the technology that supports it by providing the tools for research. From the beginning of modern science with Galileo, the time scale between discovery and application was measured in units of human life-times. Within the past thirty years, however, the unit of measure has become years, and recently even months. This exponential-like increase in the frequency of discovery and application is symptomatic of a major scale-up of intellectual activity in our lifetime. It is the scientific revolution; and the involvement of man as scientist or technologist, using the methods of science and supported by private and governmental institutions, comprises the scientific enterprise. Many of you are familiar with the frequently quoted fact that more than 95 per cent of all scientists throughout civilization are now alive and working today. This scaling-up of intellectual activity, combined with the expectations of the scientists themselves, has created an atmosphere that is both stimulating and frightening for the thoughtful investigator. As a consequence, there emerge areas of what we call, in popular language, "big science." More and more frequently, collaboration among scientists in well-developed laboratories becomes essential in an ever increasing number of disciplines—and there is no evidence that this trend will be reversed.

It is an essential feature of our university that research remains wholly within its walls and accessible to its students. The struggle that many of us face is how to preserve, and keep in view of our students, the essentially individualistic and fragile character of discovery under these circumstances of modern science. If we should fail to do so, there is no hope for undergraduate participation. But I believe we are not failing. To be specific, I might use a more recent example and one closest to my current interests, namely, experiments in space, to seek the origin of cosmic rays and to find, for example, the ways by which nature accelerates a simple hydrogen atom to an energy that is more than one billion times greater than the highest energy achieved by man-made accelerators. Obviously such problems require a mixture of theoretical and experimental training. The phenomena occur on a scale-size much greater than that of the earth and cannot be scaled down to the framework of the laboratory or the earth. Consequently, we must make the solar system our laboratory, using space probes and satellites to carry our instruments. Immediately this becomes big science; immediately we discover that we need help. Obviously it is necessary to have a professional group to follow through on the necessary equipment and the launching and tracking of various probes and satellites. And we have found it possible for students to collaborate successfully, intimately, and effectively, in these enterprises through their contributions to the definition of the experiments, theory, the buildup of the prototype experiment, and, later, in the interpretation and analysis of the results. They do not fall into the trap of becoming super-technicians, which would be the case if one attempted such efforts solely with the support of students as more or less slave labor. With the help of graduate students, we encourage selected undergraduates to work with us, learning to carry out specific assignments and later assuming some independence. Frequently these students make significant contributions. It is interesting to note, by examining the papers published by the laboratory, that undergraduates frequently are acknowledged for contributions to research. For each young man or woman it meant more than that. It meant that he had found a channel by which he could transfer what he understood from his classes to the real world of scientific research. He also learned in the laboratory that the top two or three undergraduates are invited to the weekly discussions between the senior investigator and his graduate students. By the time they are seniors in the college they are behaving like graduate students. This is a very pleasing effect to observe because it means they are getting the feel for conducting research. They also learn why this enterprise demands discipline.

There are other examples, which already exist on campus, and I would like to draw your attention to a few of them. They are found in the Department of Chemistry summer honors program under Nien-Chen Yang, or in the Institute for the Study of Metals with Russell J. Donnelley, or in the Enrico Fermi Institute with Roger H. Hildebrand. In the Division of the Biological Sciences, I understand that some plans are under way to encourage student participation in research. The essential feature of what I have described is faculty participation in an arrangement that is *mutually* beneficial and stimulating to students and faculty. This is not an exercise. It complements the proposals for independent study, or research for honors, which have been proposed by some of the faculty for honor students. But in most respects so far, these are informal arrangements. Most of the students find their way into the laboratories because they need financial support or because in an interview they appear to be attractive risks. These arrangements could form a pilot study for deeper involvement of selected undergraduate students with the frontiers of research under the faculties of the university. Not all of my colleagues agree with me. Some note that their work is not amenable to undergraduate participation. Some even feel they do not want to see the undergraduates around because it must, of necessity, mean an additional load, and to gain appreciation and understanding of their research requires an extended graduate background.

It would be surprising indeed, however, if one could not find some peripheral problems of interest and of importance that could be examined from simple points of view by our best and most highly motivated students.

It seems clear that if the college were to move toward an *open recognition of these objectives,* it would be necessary:

First, to identify the areas of research and the individuals on the faculty who have research suitable for participation and who are enthusiastic. A rough estimate within the

Department of Physics alone indicates that approximately 20 highly motivated students could be accommodated from the junior and senior classes.

Second, to develop a mechanism for acquainting students with these opportunities, including those who might otherwise not come to our university. I emphasize this point because this perhaps may represent the most important qualitative difference between one college and another college in the future.

Third, to decide whether there should be formal recognition for these activities within the four-year structure of the college.

Fourth, to provide funds where necessary, so as not to discriminate against students who otherwise have to work for income in order to stay within the college. Here I would like to point out that most laboratories are able to support such modest requirements on the legitimate basis that they are contributing to the research.

Fifth, to establish a method for evaluating the degree of success of the effort after a reasonable time. Some modest institutional arrangement should be made to take care of an ongoing effort based on these principles.

In closing my remarks, I would like briefly to return to the more difficult problem of the student in the non-science areas attempting to understand the goals, methods, and the beauty of science. Quite clearly we need to bring the knowledge of science into the areas of the humanities and social sciences wherever there is a clear relevance. It is important to give students an intimate acquaintance with some area of science and sufficiently involve them in the language of science. Wherever this is impractical, then at least the *impact of science on the human condition* forms a framework for uniting the disciplines. We might begin with Bacon, whose original aspirations in his *Novum Organum* were for science for the betterment of the human condition. Both the sciences and the arts arise from a common base, *namely, a deep human need,* and a great deal more might be done to convey the nature of science and technology as they touch upon other areas of human endeavor.

In the sciences we don't talk much about it, but there is a deep commitment to the betterment of man. Much effort by the scientific community is devoted to political and social questions so that war will never again play its historical role. It was at the University of Chicago in 1945 that Eugene Rabinowich, David Hill, and I drafted a statement of principles for the scientific community based upon our concern and worries during the war years 1944–45. *Life* magazine graciously gave us a couple of pages in October, 1945, for this statement, from which I would like to read one part which I believe stands today as a reasonable statement of the feelings of the scientific community on these matters: "The scientists do not aspire to political leadership, but having helped man make the first step into this new world, they have the responsibility of warning and advising him until he has become aware of its perils, as well as its wonders. They have lived with the secret of the atom bomb for several years; they have thought about its future and implications for mankind long before the rest of the world had become aware of the problem. It is their duty, conscious as they are of the danger which atomic power brings to mankind, and, first of all, to their own nation and their own families, to carry the warning of this danger to all people of our country and to all other nations on Earth. They must persuade all political and social groups in the country that here is a threat to the very existence of us all . . . the problem of survival cannot be postponed or disposed of by wishful thinking or the application of old, political formulas." Although this was stated with respect to nuclear weapons, I think in large measure you will see in the actions of the scientific community the same spirit today and the same desire to play a role in public affairs, insofar as they carry the tone of the above statement. Surely there are ways by which the betterment of the human condition could be better understood by knitting the contributions of science with the historical study of human values, without tampering with the inadequacies of our institutional arrangements—and in so doing the non-science students will learn about the scientific endeavor.

I'm afraid that we have not been very smart in approaching these problems, especially those of us in the sciences; they remain an open challenge to the college if it hopes to develop civilized men and women.

DIVERSITY

John R. Platt

I celebrate diversity. Our research, our lives, our goals, our pursuit of excellence are all too homogeneous. La Roche-foucauld writes: "God has put as many differing talents in man as trees in Nature: and each talent, like each tree, has its own special character and aspect. . . . The finest pear tree in the world cannot produce the most ordinary apple, and the most splendid talent cannot duplicate the effect of the homeliest skill."

I think he means that other men are not like him in being able to make maxims of this kind. But what he says is true. How many of us have been given Ds and Fs in apple-tree courses simply because the teacher was too narrow to see that we had to be nurtured as pear trees? Progress would be faster and life more interesting if we pursued more diverse goals—goals of excellence to be sure, but goals of our own, different from what everybody else is pursuing—and if we tolerated and encouraged the same sort of individuality in others. I want life to be various. I want to see around me not only apple trees but pear trees, not only fruit trees but slow-growing oaks and evergreen pines and rosebushes and bitter but salubrious herbs and casual dandelions and good old spread-out grass. Let us be different, and enjoy the differences!

Science and Technology

Nowhere are we as diverse as we might be. Science and technology today encompass thousands of specializations; yet it is easy to see that the specialists are probably overconcentrating on certain subjects, while other subjects, of equal interest and importance and ripeness for development, are almost entirely neglected. A short time ago it was announced that there were over four hundred government and industrial contracts and projects for studying the new device known as the optical laser, which is able to produce a peculiarly coherent and brilliant beam of light. Now this is an interesting field, but—four hundred projects! This represents several thousand scientists and engineers who have jumped, or been pushed, onto this bandwagon in the five years since the laser was invented. The motorcar was developed with less than forty manufacturing and development teams, and the whole field of atomic spectroscopy was developed in perhaps no more than forty research laboratories. One cannot help wondering whether everything important to discover in the field of lasers might not have been discovered just as fast with only forty projects, with the other three hundred and sixty groups doing something less repetitious. One suspects that many of the four hundred projects might not have been started if their leaders had known in advance —before they got their grant money and could not back out—that they would be competing with 399 others.

Over the past twenty-five years, I have changed my own field from physics and chemistry to biology, and in every field of science I have seen there are areas that are being overstudied in this way by men who might be doing something more valuable with their brains. There is not only bandwagoning, there is nitpicking, where a multiplying succession of scientists pursues more and more ingrown exercises in what were originally interesting and important subjects. I am polite and will not name all these areas. That is left as an exercise for the student. But I think there may be symptoms of overstudy in some parts of molecular chemistry, where even the insiders often admit that they are doing rather repetitious studies on rather repetitious series of molecules. And some nuclear physicists, in relaxed moments, will be heard to sigh that the research teams are too big and the apparatus too complicated and the results hardly worth the effort any more. Many physicists have changed to molecular biology, where there seems to be more novelty and more scope for individual creative achievement. But in that field also there are now complaints that too many hundreds have taken up "the DNA game" and that it is time to move on.

Many of the men in these areas will defend their studies, of course. They have ego-involvement, as they should have, and financial dependence as well. If there are many men in a subject, they can point quite accurately to many achievements, and can say quite truthfully that with more men and more money they would have had even more. The important thing they do not say is what perhaps more valuable things they might have done instead. Perhaps only the broadened administrator, or the student not yet committed, has the detachment to make a real comparison of this kind, judging the promise of different fields and their excess study or neglect.

One reason why some fields are overstudied these days is our present system of government grants. If the grand old man in a certain field was skilled at "grantsmanship" just after World War II and got large grants or contracts for a few years, he was able to feed numerous undergraduate, graduate, and postdoctoral students. As a result, within a few years he produced a dozen more trained scientists in the same field, specialists who had published papers and who knew how to apply for grants and who, as established experts, would recommend each other's grants and might even become agency officials. And from these trained scientists, a new generation of students has of course multiplied again, and international conferences must be held in this area of rapidly growing importance. It is a chain reaction. Even the undergraduates can see how important the subject is, with all those visiting lecturers passing through and praising each other.

Meanwhile that poor old area where the senior scientist lagged in applying for his first grant a few years ago is still trying to catch up, but is falling farther and farther behind in money and manpower, regardless of its importance or equal promise of success.

I am exaggerating slightly, of course. Students do change subjects; and new discoveries are made which open up new fields. But the tendency is clear, and some fields will be overstudied and others will be neglected as long as government granting agencies refuse to make value judgments between areas, and say, in effect, that whatever many scientists want to do—that is, whatever they were supported for learning to do as students twenty years ago—must be the thing most worth doing and worth supporting.

I think there are thousands of scientists who would like to change to less crowded and more interesting fields if they thought the change would not be disapproved and if they could plan how to make a living and how to get research support while making the change. I think this would be a good thing. Mobility spreads the skills in a labor market, and mobility would spread the skills in science. Kant, Helmholtz, Pasteur, all changed fields. Enrico Fermi once said that a scientist should change fields every ten years; that in the first place his ideas were exhausted by then, and he owed it to the younger men in the field to let them advance; and that in the second place his ideas might still be of great value in bringing a fresh viewpoint to a different field. If government agencies do not want to point the finger at some areas as being overcrowded, they might at least consider giving wide publicity to the relative numbers of men and projects in different areas and to the ranking of the importance or promise of these areas by experts from near-by fields; and they might be able to take the lead in pointing out *under*studied fields and in soliciting grant applications in such fields.

Are there understudied fields? There certainly are, and interesting ones too. In the field of the colors of molecular compounds, in which I have done some work, there must be hundreds of scientists studying the spectra of diatomic gases for NASA and the Air Force, and thousands of scientists studying the spectra of benzenes and petroleum compounds and dyes for the oil and dye and photographic industries; but only one or two laboratories have made systematic studies of the spectra of the flower pigments, and I have been able to find only one paper in English on the absorption spectra of the irises of our own eyes. These subjects are difficult, but no more so than many others that are avidly pursued; and they are of considerable biological and genetic and human interest.

Much of the work on visual pigments and on the biochemistry of vision has been done in a single laboratory, that of George Wald at Harvard University. And in spite of the journalistic excitement that was produced a few years ago by the curious color demonstrations of Edwin Land of the Polaroid Corporation, the number of scientists working on the physics and chemistry and anatomy of color perception, or indeed of any aspect of perception, is still only a handful. The molecular basis of memory—what molecules are involved in the growth of nervous connections among the brain cells when we learn something—is the subject of articles in *The New York Times* every week or two, but there are scarcely more than a dozen laboratories where such studies are being pursued. And the mechanisms of photosynthesis, in spite of their human and biological and economic importance for feeding the world, are probably being studied seriously at no more than about twenty laboratories, and the subject is still almost untouched by the powerful methods of the DNA revolution.

Marine biology—the problem of understanding the odd creatures of the sea and their development and cycles and diseases—is something done at only a few centers on the coasts, many of them poorly staffed, although its importance to the life of the world should make it a matter for basic study by the best physicists, chemists, and biologists everywhere. I once heard the president of a midwest university say that this was not a proper subject for emphasis at an inland school—even though his astronomers were working in both hemispheres, his cosmic-ray men had networks around the world, and his engineers were readying apparatus for solar system orbits from what is now Cape Kennedy. He was not inland except to marine biology. It is not our geography that is inland, it is our failure to understand the untouched diversity of really important things that are crying out to be done.

We badly need new tools of research that almost no one is working on. A recent theoretical study has suggested that it might be possible to make improved electron microscopes that would permit seeing individual atoms or identifying a molecule directly just by looking at it. The importance of this for organic chemistry or biology may be imagined. It might be as great as the importance of the original electron microscope. But the number of qualified investigators who have applied for grants to try to develop such improved microscopes can be counted on the fingers of one hand. The development of research tools is not a traditional business of biology as it is of physics, and this and many other types of tools—such as new types of centrifuge, new methods of sectioning and staining and visualizing tissues, and new methods for automating genetic studies—are lagging because of the lack of scientists who will turn aside to develop them and the inability of our laboratories to assign task forces to these important projects, as they could easily do if it were a matter of military or space studies.

One of the hopes of some of the scientists who have been working on the development of automatic vehicles for the scientific exploration of the surface of Mars has been that such vehicles would require the development of a completely automated chemical and biological laboratory for studying small samples of material. Chemistry and biochemistry have lagged behind other fields in applying computers and automation methods to laboratory analysis and synthesis. Students still pour liquids back and forth by hand and sit watching flasks boil as they did in the time of the alchemists. An automated lab might change all this, with incalculable consequences in making our chemical and biochemical studies faster and simpler and more accurate, but we do not seem to be able to undertake such important developments except in connection with some extraneous goal such as the space project.

There are lags, and understudied subjects, around many fields of science just because of the narrowness of training in the fields themselves. In astronomy, many of the great developments of the last century have come from outside the field, including the analysis of ionization in stellar atmospheres, the idea of nuclear reactions in the stars, radio astronomy, astrochemistry, magnetohydrodynamics, and the discovery of synchrotron radiation. Astronomers have tended to be ingrown, trained only by other astronomers and isolated in observatories away from the flux of new ideas in physics and chemistry, and they have often resisted such innovations.

In medicine also, many of the most fundamental advances have been made, not by doctors, but by physicists and chemists and biochemists. Witness the germ theory, the development of many antibiotics, and the DNA story, not to mention technical tools like X-rays and radiation, the electron microscope, and radioactive tracers. There are exceptions, but all too often the training of young medical research men is a training in repetition rather than in the important new methods and ideas of biology and the other sciences. As one wit has said, "We learn exactly what we are taught. Send a man to jail for four years and he becomes a trained criminal. Send him to medical school for four years and he becomes self-important and incurious." It is an overstatement but it has a core of truth.

Outside the sciences, philosophy is another field that is too ingrown. It suffers from being taught by philosophers. Many of the major new philosophical ideas of the last one hundred years—creative evolution, pragmatism, empiricism, logical positivism, personalism—have come, not from philosophy but from the sciences, evolution, psychology, mathematics, and physics. Diversity, diversity! There are probably many other areas that I have not mentioned, where the narrowness of training by the professionals with their ingrown ideas is evidently an actual handicap to progress in the field.

On the technological side, we develop some things well and other things not at all. We send men into orbit and we can fly faster than sound, but our clothes are in many ways inferior to those of a bird. The technical design of clothes is still prehistoric, in spite of synthetic fibers and sewing machines. The fibers must still be drawn out like animal or plant fibers, then spun, then woven or knitted, and then cut or sewn more or less to fit, just as they have been for thousands of years. And then these threads do not protect us against rain or cold, or shade or ventilate us in the hot sun, unless we put on and take off many layers, which we must carry around in a suitcase. Why should I not have a single suit that would shed rain and that I could ruffle up for comfort in any weather, like the feathers of a bird? It is because no one—not even the Army, which might be expected to have the greatest interest in it—has put a task force on the problem of designing clothing material of variable porosity and variable thermal conductivity which could be molded to the body. Not everybody would want a single universal suit, but it would be nice to have the option. It might not even be very hard to invent. But we still have prehistoric patterns of thought in what touches us most closely. Helicopters, *si;* clothes, *no.*

It is the same story with shoes, which are still sewn of pieces of leather or plastic. And with housing, which lags far behind automobile technology and still has piece-by-piece assembly and leaking roofs and windows and no standard modular connection to the needed city services.

It is as though we had collective taboos against certain types of development, like the taboo against work on oral contraceptives before about 1950, or the refusal to consider or finance Buckminster Fuller's geodesic dome buildings until the Army used the principle for radomes, or the reluctance of psychologists and physiologists to study sleep before the work of Nathaniel Kleitman and his co-workers made it respectable. Scientists are not really innovators, and neither are industrial companies and government agencies and their research-and-development teams. They all shrink, like other men, from unheard-of projects for which there is no precedent, even obvious and important projects, because they are afraid they will be laughed at or lose their support.

As psychologists once backed away from the study of sleep, so biologists and doctors today back away from the study of regeneration and rejuvenation, although the central importance of these studies to human welfare is obvious. They sound too much like science fiction—as though every development today did not!—and they have often been given a bad name by sensational reports like those of the monkey gland studies of the 1920's. But lower animals can regenerate parts of their bodies. Lobsters can regenerate claws; and newts, which are vertebrates much farther up the scale, can still regenerate eyes and optic nerves. It seems that the power to do this is not lost in the higher animals but is only "turned off" or economized somehow, since we still have the full information for our embryological development preserved in every cell of our adult bodies. A concentrated study of "tissue inducers" or of the restoration of embryonic biochemistry might permit a useful measure of regeneration, and the discovery of how to do it might take only a fraction of the biologist years now being spent on minor studies of DNA. A man who had lost a finger or a hand might find it very useful to grow not merely skin over the stump, but bones and muscles, even if it took just as long as growing the original finger or hand. But we will never know whether it can be done until a few dozen scientists get to work on it.

Likewise with rejuvenation, or the preservation or restoration of sexual activity and of other youthful functions after the age of fifty or so. About 20 per cent of the people of the world are in this age group, and so this is a problem affecting the health and marital happiness of more than six hundred million people. Some of the processes of aging that cause us to run down may be programmed innately into our genetic apparatus, while others may be due simply to the breakdown of certain repair mechanisms. Could these genetic programs be reversed or delayed? Or could the repair mechanisms be replaced? The answers are not certain, but there are many avenues to try, and it seems to me quite possible that the work of a few hundred biologists in this important area might do more for the daily happiness of hundreds of millions of people than even a successful solution of the terrible problems of cancer and heart disease; yet the number of researchers in this field is probably not 1 per cent of the number in the cancer field. We are driven by the fear of death, not by an interest in living more abundantly. Who would have the courage and love of humanity to try to organize an American Rejuvenation Society as rich as the American Cancer Society for the support of research? The jokesters would have a field day. And so the important thing does not get done.

There are other possible experiments that use the same biological principles and that would be extremely interesting to try, even though they are still more "far out." Since the nucleus of every adult cell in the body contains all the genetic information necessary for copying the complete adult, could we not take out some of these nuclei with a micropipette and insert one of them in a fertilized egg cell in place of the egg's own nucleus, letting the egg cell then develop and grow up into an identical twin of the original adult?

J. B. Gurdon of Oxford has already succeeded in doing this with frogs. If this procedure will work for higher animals, it could be the basis of a new animal-copying industry. One can imagine cells being taken from a prize cow or from a champion race-horse, and the nuclei from them being transplanted into newly fertilized egg cells and the egg cells reimplanted into a foster mother or several foster mothers, producing several calves or foals, which would all be identical twins of the champion. It could be a profitable business! And a few years later, if we wanted to have a dozen new George Beadles or a dozen new deans just like Wayne Booth, we could just shake their hands and take away a few unneeded skin cells. And we could take the nuclei of those cells and transplant them into some fertilized egg cells of some young ladies who had to get rid of them; and then reimplant these improved cells in women who had always wanted just this kind of children; and in nine months there would be a dozen beautiful babies in Hyde Park looking just like George Beadle or Wayne Booth.

The implantation of egg cells into foster mothers is already being done today. The only difference here is that it might be done now not with randomly mixed genetic material but with highly selected genetic material of known capabilities. Lots of mothers might want to see what they could do if they could try over, in bringing up some of the great characters of the world. The identical twins in different homes might enable us to find out for the first time how much of human achievement is due to heredity and how much to environment. And in twenty-five years, we could have the greatest collection of young nuclear physicists, or violinists, or biologists, or deans in the world.

It would also be useful to try animal-copying with the nucleus taken from one species and the egg in which it was implanted taken from another. Donkey and horse can be mated; will a donkey nucleus in a horse egg-cell give a donkey—or something more like a mule? This might teach us something about the developmental embryonic differences between species. If it would work, we might be able to save some vanishing species by transplanting their cell nuclei

into the egg cells of foster species. Is the DNA that carries
heredity destroyed immediately when an animal dies? If not,
we might find some woolly mammoths locked for thousands
of years in the Arctic ice, and if their meat is still edible,
perhaps their DNA is still viable and might be injected, say,
into elephant egg cells, to give baby mammoths again. By
some such methods, perhaps we might achieve "paleo-recon-
struction" of the ancient Mexican corn or of "mummy
wheat," or even of the flies that are sometimes found preserved in amber. One man has devoted his life to recon-
structing creatures like the ancient Aurochs, by backcrossing
modern cattle. May not these other genetic methods of
paleo-study also be worth trying? Success is uncertain but the
rewards would be great. I see here lifetimes of fascinating
possibilities for ingenious young biologists.

These particular experiments I have listed are all connected with the fact that the nucleus of an adult cell contains all the genetic information. But there are dozens of
other areas of science that contain such families of uncon-
ventional experiments just waiting to be tried. There are the
experiments required for the selective breeding and herding
of sea animals and "farming" the oceans. There are experiments on animal development, using our new knowledge of
embryonic growth in attempts to develop larger brains or
stronger muscles. And experiments on the closer shaping of
animal behavior, not just to make trick animals for the
movies, but to make more versatile pets or better dogs for the
blind. And experiments on electronic transducers to bring
animal sounds into our range of hearing and our sounds into
their range of hearing, so as to learn whether dolphins or
chimpanzees or Siamese cats might learn to use signals and
symbols more as we do, if we made it easier for them. This
might give us a better understanding of the origins of our

own communication and linguistic development over the past few hundred thousand years.

Finally, there is an important set of experiments and developments needed for devising more sophisticated machines to serve biological functions. Not just artificial kidneys and pacemakers and artificial hearts—all of which are now under study—but balancing machines, to help the paralyzed to walk, with motors as compact and powerful and fast as our own muscles, and with feedback circuits as clever as our own balancing. Should these be so hard to devise—for men whose electronic circuits have flown past Mars transmitting pictures? Perhaps not, but the amount of scientific and engineering effort devoted by the nation to such problems is probably less than one ten-thousandth of that of the space effort.

The balancing problem is part of the interesting problem of making self-guiding automata—artificial cybernetic organisms, or "Cyborgs," as someone has called them—with pattern-perceiving sensory systems and communication systems and control programs and self-contained power sources and motor motions. Such systems will be needed for exploring the hostile surface of the moon and Mars and sending back data, but they would also be useful for exploring sea bottoms and volcanoes, and for fire-fighting and other dangerous operations. We are on the edge of understanding how to make such automata, but the problem is still being studied at only a half-dozen centers and still does not enlist the hundreds of trained and inventive minds that will be needed to make such devices work cheaply and well.

These things I have been talking about are the science fiction of a few years ago, but they are now on the verge of being technically possible, even though they are still long shots. Scientists are often embarrassed to admit that they are professionally interested in such things, and I am not sure that a man who worked on them would be recommended for promotion in many of our more conventional departments. Yet they are of journalistic interest—that is, human interest—far beyond the niggling scientific measurements that we know how to do and that lead to ordinary scientific papers and promotions. And it is not clear that their success is any more uncertain than, say, the success of fusion power, on which we have already spent hundreds of millions of dollars. No, the trouble is that these experiments that touch on our fundamental assumptions about life encounter a kind of collective unconscious scientific censorship that almost makes them more taboo than the taboos of sex. To get away from it, we will have to have scientific leaders who will rise above the taboos—as they finally did in oral contraceptives—and who will show us how to do what would be humanly interesting to do in one area after another. Perhaps the time is ripe for such leaders to appear, and perhaps they would find more support today from administrators and granting agencies than they would have found even a few years ago.

It is time for more scientific diversity. The question to be asked is no longer, "What does physics have the apparatus and the equations for?" but rather "What are the curious things in the world?" "And what are the needs of man?"

Social and Economic Diversity

But science is not the only area of life where we pursue some lines excessively while neglecting others. It happens throughout our economic and social life as well, and commonly the reason is again the coupling of money to conventional patterns of tradition and taboo. Galbraith has emphasized that the private sector of the economy is vigorous while the public sector languishes. But even the private sector is not as diversely effective as it might be.

Thus, we have automobiles in plenty—and I am no longer one of those who complain about their design. Archaeologists eventually may rate them as our handsomest artifacts. They are remarkably functional and economical and satisfying—and some day they may even be safe! But why should we continue indefinitely to be blocked from having the same kind of technological skill and competitive economy in the construction of our houses? Or even in our chairs and sofas? These are items that are less than one-hundredth as complex as an automobile but may cost one-fifth as much, even though they are sold in comparable numbers.

And why should the cars have to pass over such ugly streets and highways, which are paid for by the same motorists who choose the cars? To speak of the worst of the eyesores, almost every vista in America is made hideous by wooden gallows poles and dangling suspender lines of the power companies. A $30,000 home or a $10 million building may have its view defaced from all directions, looking in or looking out, because of a half-dozen $500 power poles whose sole excuse for the intrusion is supposedly commercial or civic economy. I think the daily hideousness of these objects is one of the things that makes us insensitive to other forms of neighborhood blight. Channel some of our dynamic economic energy into removing the poles, and I suspect many lesser uglinesses would be swept away in a wave of neighborhood beautification.

Could we not have more diversity in our patterns of houses and lots? If we put our houses at the edge of the streets, facing inward on the block, the houses could all look onto a sizable little park in the middle of the block, with trees and a fountain and swings and a place for oldsters to sit and for children to play safely away from the street. Give us the pleasure of facing our very own park, and who would prefer the useless luxury of separate private lots, half of whose area is never used?

I think we should also explore different family and neighborhood patterns. Ask people who have traveled and lived in many different types of communities where in their lives they have been happiest and enjoyed life the most. Surprisingly often the answer is in some form of group living. Many Englishmen have said it was in their student days at Oxford that they first learned the "sheer delight" of living. For others it might be a kibbutz, or even perhaps a hitch in the Navy on a good ship. Physicists and chemists still talk about the wartime colony at Los Alamos where they learned to share life because they could not talk about their work. For Chicago graduates, it was the old Howarth House co-operative with its intellectual explorations and taste of freedom. Many a Chicago faculty family still looks back with nostalgia to the years in the "pre-fabs" on Fifty-eighth Street or on Sixtieth Street after the war.

Listening to these shared recollections, one realizes that we are basically tribal creatures, and one begins to wonder whether our conventional pattern of life today, with its separate households and separated age groups, is really giving us the full satisfactions of living. The "pre-fabs" were clusters of two-story buildings around a central court, and they were shabby and crowded and noisy. But in the court, a dozen small children could play safely. Older children could walk to kindergarten and the Lab Schools. The men and many of the women worked or studied within a few blocks and spent little time commuting. And though there was solitude and anonymity for those who wished it, the currents of the world passed through, and there was always conversation, with couples dropping in for spaghetti and wine, or going to political meetings or to plays and movies.

Good living is shared with a tribe. At the Marine Biological Laboratories at Woods Hole, Massachusetts, where I have spent several summers, the boundaries between the generations seem to disappear, as well as the boundaries between work and play and between indoors and outdoors and between man and environment. Children and students and teachers walk barefoot in and out of the laboratories, arguing science and studying the odd creatures brought up from the sea. All night they watch the fish embryos developing in the dishes, and they go out before dawn together to catch the big striped bass. The four-year-olds solemnly examine frogs, the ten-year-olds sell their catch of dogfish to the labs, the fifteen-year-olds listen to the DNA arguments on the beach or play savage tennis with the senior scientists. No wonder they all want to turn into marine biologists!

Why should we not make environments for ourselves where we can have this kind of diversity and human satisfaction and pleasure of living all year around, instead of just in a student community or a wartime colony or a summer laboratory? I think that many universities and laboratories are neglecting one of their greatest potential attractions, in not trying to arrange environments so that living intellectual communities of this sort could spring up around them. Make a good faculty center for easy and informal interactions, with faculty apartments and guest houses and conference rooms and lounges and terraces and recreation space and dining rooms and theaters, and the intellectual dialogue would never stop.

We need more diverse types of communities, and more diverse types of schools—a subject we will come back to in a moment—and more diversity in politics and government. It is not generally realized that half the members of the United States Congress are lawyers, even though lawyers are no more than one-half of 1 per cent of the general population. Such an overrepresentation would have horrified the makers of the Constitution, who anticipated that Congress would consist largely of landowners and leading merchants and professional men like themselves. I think it is easy to see that the present situation has come about not because we prefer lawyers as our representatives but because they are the only group with a strong economic incentive for going into politics in great numbers. A lawyer, unlike an engineer or merchant or any other type of candidate, adds to his professional knowledge by being a candidate, and his partners handle his cases for him while he is in office, and he brings them business and comes back afterward with enhanced professional value and useful professional information. It is no surprise that lawyers run for office!

But without wishing to belittle the many good lawyers who are our elected representatives, I think this collective overconcentration of one professional group in our legislatures, even a group that is expert in the laws, is undesirable. Lawyers tend to come from a relatively narrow economic group and their training is also rather narrow, being weak, for example, in the modern psychology and biology that they ought to have, and in the science and technology that are changing the world. It may be their training that is partly responsible for much of our congressional pettifoggery and oratory and black-and-white opinions, and for a tendency to emphasize legalisms and punishment rather than constructive development. The very different approach of the handful of teachers in Congress is especially marked. Diversity, I say! Let us find a way to reduce the financial sacrifices involved in running for office, so that we can have a Congress not only of lawyers but of teachers, scientists, doctors, engineers, businessmen, farmers, ministers, social workers, labor leaders, managers of co-operatives, and housewives. Let us have a body that can speak more accurately for the full range of interests and groups that make up America.

Diversity in Education

But finally and most importantly, we need more diversity in education. Students today can hardly realize how much the alternatives available to them have been closed up by zealous professional professors in the last thirty years. In the 1930's, the colleges knew they had been liberalized by John Dewey, and they offered what is now sneered at as a "cafeteria system" of education. Yet what delightful explorations it permitted us! When I was an undergraduate physics major at Northwestern University, I not only took physics and math courses, but I had time and electives to take two years of French and three years of German, including Goethe and Schiller, plus astronomy, economics, philosophy, public speaking, music, and a seminar on the origins of war.

Our present survey courses are more thorough and systematic, but not so tailored to the individual curiosity and enthusiasm. Many colleges have pushed electives almost entirely out of the curriculum, so that they will have time for so-called honors programs. All too often, they should be called "narrows programs," for what they make is one-dimensional men.

It particularly worries me that physics and chemistry and other science majors have now lost most of their free electives. Scientists are now rising to executive positions in business and industry and are major international and military advisors. About one-third of all physicists eventually become administrators. I do not want a world, and I do not think any sane person wants a world, in which the major decisions on technological and military and international affairs are made by one-dimensional men, men who have never had time to explore art or music or history or philosophy or literature or the non-technical achievements of mankind!

Many of the once-great liberal arts colleges are narrowing their honors programs just like everybody else. How else do you think they get all those graduate fellowships? The ironic thing is that the graduate schools say that this kind of speed-up only gives these students an edge for about six months and that by the end of the first year the other men who have not had this undergraduate graduate stuff may be doing just as well. The rat race is useless, even in its own terms—except for getting those golden pelletships at the end of the box.

The only thing that saves us is that the good students learn many things outside the curriculum. In fact I think that in many cases the reputation of these hard-driving schools, both the high schools and the colleges, is not due to the courses or the staff at all, but is due to the quality of the students they are able to get. If you have hotshots, it makes little difference what you teach them—or whether you teach them at all; they will find out from each other (as the whole human race did!) how to be great contributors to society. The importance of this initial student selection factor has never been sorted out in assessing our schools. Many a school has good graduates, not because its education is good, but because its students were good when they came in and have not been much damaged.

Even so, the hotshot dimension is not the only one to emphasize. In my experience, the demanding teacher who talks about excellence is frequently the one who believes that all students can be ranked on a single scale, an exam scale or an I.Q. scale, as either good or bad. Why should we assume or insist that our students have only one important dimension of variation? I want rosebushes in my classes, and some persevering oak trees. Chicago has been fortunate to have men like Jacob Getzels and Philip Jackson who have emphasized that there is another dimension of creativity in students that has little relation to I.Q.

We do not even allow for the physiological variations in students. Students, like professors, are not all wakeful or sleepy at the same time. We often start by trying to teach them things when they—and we—are half-asleep; and then we try to get them to go to sleep when they are wide awake. Many a child's dislike of school may simply reflect his parents' dislike of those awful hours and the half-awake bickering breakfasts before he gets off in the morning. Would it be so impossible to have an education at one time of day for skylarks and at another time for nightingales? Even professors might like it. Some of the world's greatest leaders napped in the daytime and worked around the clock. Classes in the evening might lead to the best discussions of all if you could sleep in the morning. I have never understood why these possibilities are not seriously examined by educators who are supposed to know something about the psychology and physiology of learning.

While we are speaking of the right to physiological diversity, let us not forget the right of some of the students to be women. It is easy to show that prejudices and handicaps to women's education still abound. Fathers send sons to college rather than daughters; and not only fathers but deans will cut off a college girl's financial support if she gets married, where they would not cut off a boy's. I have known professors in several departments, even at Chicago, who refused to take girls as graduate students on the ground that they would probably get married and not use the education. The nepotism rules of many schools result in failure to hire good women teachers if they have the misfortune to be married to good men teachers, so that the image of the woman intellectual the student sees is always that of a woman who has renounced marriage. A great midwest university lost a great woman scientist in this way, through refusing to pay her a salary separate from her husband's—until she became famous!

What is worse, however, is that the colleges and counselors do nothing to combat the double standard of the college men, who may learn far-out things in biology or anthropology but are never shaken out of their conventional station-wagon images of what marriage should be. They go on assuming that the college wife, or the graduate wife, is the one who shops and cooks and cleans, even if she is carrying courses and trying to do equal work. The delights of student equality extend to men rooming together or to women rooming together, but not to a man and wife in the same apartment. The result of this conventional image—which the girls have often picked up as well as the men—is that American women are concentrating on conventional and subordinate jobs and that, compared to women of other countries, they are making fewer and fewer contributions to our national life, either as educators or editors or scientists or doctors or lawyers or judges or legislators or political leaders. There are fewer women in the United States Congress today than there were thirty years ago—or than there are now in Pakistan, where women just recently took off the veil! We are only getting half-power out of our educated and intellectual women, and it impoverishes us all.

Poverty, Austerity, and Overwork

To come back to the narrowing pressures on student life in general, I think it is not at all clear that the intellectual and the economic pressures on students today are either good education or good economics. Students are probably the most overworked and underpaid class in our society. Their training has now been shown by many studies to be the most important element in the economic development and prosperity of a country, and yet they are not paid as well as their brothers who become plumbers' apprentices. The eighteen-year-old brother or sister who works in a factory or store gets off at five o'clock and has enough income to have an apartment and a car and books and records and recreation and a paid vacation. He can have guests in and can come in or go out at any hour. Even the brother in the Army has good pay and limited hours of duty. But the student is treated, not like his brothers or parents or teachers, but like a monk, with a vow of poverty, austerity, and overwork—a vow which is not even his own vow, but has been taken for him. He works until ten or midnight or later at subjects his brothers might never master, and he is supposed to get money from his family or borrow it or to be grateful for a fellowship that still leaves him below the poverty level. He is frequently locked in at night and forbidden to have a car or an apartment and has little money for his own books or for good meals or concerts. He is given cafeteria fare in cinderblock buildings and never learns to live like a human being. It is an affluent-society parody of medieval monasticism, with the universities—the primary sources of new economic development today—treated as priestly beggars, and with the professors themselves, who have grown up in the system, approving this treatment of the students, and feeling, always, that they have too much money and do not work hard enough.

It is a funny four-year gap in our economic scheme. Students are overworked and underpaid undoubtedly because they are the only group in our society which is too old for child labor laws to protect them and too young to have a union or professional market competition—as their parents and their professors have—to help them get more civilized hours and treatment.

And oh, how long those hours are that we are forcing on ambitious students in good high schools and colleges today! You professors who have measured the rates of learning, have you measured the optimum number of hours for intellectual work? Do they agree with the standard homework assignment? It is estimated that a medical student is expected to learn 30,000 bits of information in his first year, or 100 bits a day, if he obeys every demand of the instructors. Is it actually possible to learn at this rate, or does this not simply overload the brain and block any real organization of the material? No wonder the drop-out and failure rate is high. No wonder the suicide rate is high.

Men do not become wise and full by studying fourteen hours a day, or ten hours a day, and possibly not even eight hours a day. This is not education for the good life or the good society. There is a limit to the human capacity to pack in new knowledge just as there is a limit to the capacity of a stuffed goose. The limit may be no more than a few hours before we need a change of pace for the rest of the day, a period of exercise or recreation or idleness, eating and chatting, in order for us to assimilate new information and fit it together.

The trouble is that the faculty itself still thinks that this is the only way of education. The student is not taught how to be broad and human because the faculty frequently does not know how to be broad and human. *Nemo dat quod non habet*. No one can give what he does not have. The student is overloaded with information because the professor is overloaded with information, with a piled-up desk and a bulging briefcase. He does not know how to handle it himself, and so he passes it on. And many a professor equates education with judgments and grades. I have heard of one man, a sweet man in his personal life, who gave out seven Fs in a class of twenty-five undergraduate majors because some students were either not prepared for his three-hour course or were unwilling to spend twenty hours a week on it; and because he did not have the perception or the humanity to tell them earlier that they should not be in the course. This little piece of self-righteousness will cost these unfortunates hundreds of thousands of dollars in lost fellowships and graduate education and potential job opportunities over their lifetimes. In any other line of work, this man could be sued. In a university, he tells his colleagues it shows how poor the students are today, and they cluck sympathetically. Education is to lead forth; but such a man evidently thinks that leading is damning. Sometimes such men mellow as they mature, but all too often these black-and-white academics only get more and more self-righteous all the way to retirement.

The student comes for teaching and what he gets is grades. We are hypnotized by grades. They seem so exact and discussable. I have seen departments where one-quarter of the teachers' time and energy was spent in making up exams and grading them. If any administration doubts this, let it measure the ratio. This amount of time spent with individual students could have pulled many of them over the border-line; but we prefer to retreat to written questions. It gives us renewed proof that our students are one dimensional. What Montessori said should be written in letters of fire: "The business of a teacher is to teach, not to judge." The business of a professor is to give, not grades, but intellectual contagion.

Do not misunderstand my criticisms here. I think the academic life can be the most varied and imaginative and interesting life in the world, and I love it. But I am talking about its distortions and how they narrow it from what it might become. Its great men are so very great and its little men are so little. And it pains me when I see one of those academic men who has deliberately narrowed himself to an intellectual pinpoint and has cut off all that life might be. It pains me when I see a man so buried in his work that he hardly remembers how to read or talk about anything else or how to treat his wife or his children with humanity and interest, or even how to take a vacation. Emerson must have been thinking of such men when he said: "The state of society is one in which the members have suffered amputation from the trunk, and strut about so many walking monsters—a good finger, a neck, a stomach, an elbow, but never a man."

The academic world is perhaps no worse in this respect than the world of government or the world of business, but it is sad all the same. The teacher is the one man who most needs to know what it is to be a complete man with wholeness and diversity and humor; for when his vision is distorted, the vision of a whole generation may be warped.

I think it is time to say loudly and clearly that the interval of higher education should be an interval of learning to live like cultured human beings instead of like monks and academics. Let us begin to use this time in a new way. Let us begin to explore less conventionally. Let us begin to have equal rights for our differences. Along with excellence let us have diversity. Instead of overload and punishment, let us have excitement and leadership. Let us try to find ways in which students can be given the money and leisure they ought to have as valuable apprentices in an affluent society. Let us bring up a generation of young adults full of the delight of living, interested in many things, and knowing not only how to be intellectual but how to be full and creative men.

The Second Educational Revolution

I think that this goal I have suggested, of trying to make the college years more humane, more cultured, and more diverse, is just part of a new educational revolution that will totally change the structure of our schools in the next twenty years. This revolution may be even more thoroughgoing than the revolution that was made by John Dewey and the other reformers seventy years ago, when they swept out the obsolete and stuffy classical education of the nineteenth century and redefined the goals of education as education for society and education for living.

Today our education has indeed become an excellent education for our society, so far as its professional content is concerned, but it is still obsolete and clumsy in its teaching methods. Since World War II, a revolution has occurred in information and communication and in our knowledge of the biology and psychology of the brain and the psychology of learning. It is beginning to be urgent for us to adapt our educational system to take account of these advances. Mass education up until now has been hard and punitive, with more of the stick than of the carrot. It has been hardest and most punitive in the colleges, where many departments and schools are still proud to have standards so strict that they flunk out one-third of their freshmen.

But it is now possible to move away from this traditional pattern. It has become clear that the psychology of positive reinforcement, of encouraged curiosity and reward, works much better than the psychology of negative reinforcement, as great teachers have always known. As the psychologist Lawrence Kubie says, "Efficient learning is never hard." We do not teach football by giving exams, but by contagion, and the students learn it and play it spontaneously. Why should we teach Chaucer differently? Students and faculty did not crowd the halls to hear Agassiz lecture, or A. J. Carlson or Fermi, just because they were going to get an exam on it later. If a school is so unlucky that it does not have a teacher of Chaucer or of Western civilization or of physics who can teach by contagion, let us give the students leave to go to some other subject where we do have such a man. The enthusiasm of learning and of discovering for oneself is more important to the university and to the student and to his final performance in society than any particular coverage of subject matter.

The new psychology has brought us new discoveries and new methods. At the University of Chicago, Benjamin Bloom and others have emphasized the effect of early enrichment, and of preschool tutoring at ages one to four, on later I.Q. and school success. We now have programmed electric type-writers to teach reading and writing to children of two to four as well as to retarded readers, and the new ITA phonetic alphabet is speeding up early reading in its own way. At higher grades, the discovery of the power of rapid-reinforcement methods offers new ease and success. Programmed learning and teaching machines and "Tutortexts" offer the student individual instruction in which he can go at his own pace, and they promise to make spelling and geography and physics and anatomy and other subjects both easier and more quickly mastered.

In high school, the new PSSC courses in physics and the others like them in mathematics and chemistry and biology have made a revolution across the nation in the teaching of science, and efforts are well under way to create science programs with the same exciting immediacy all the way down to the kindergarten level. In fact it now appears that the difficulty with many subjects is that we have been teaching them too late—as though we waited until eighteen to begin to teach reading and writing! Often the seven-year-old can learn about sets and binary arithmetic and rates of change and the difference between mass and weight more easily than the college sophomore. The main difficulty is the problem of teaching the second-grade teacher to understand these subjects!

These remarkable new methods, however, have not yet been drawn together into a unified educational approach. We have a better engine, a better transmission, and a better steering mechanism, but they have not yet been fitted together to make a complete car. It seems very likely that when they are all put together, these new developments in education will reinforce each other and will make possible further gains that would not come from any one alone. Preschool reading and writing would make room for beginning science in the early grades. Binary arithmetic in the second grade may make a child ready and eager for number theory and computer programming in the sixth. Rates of change at age seven will permit an easy introduction to economics at age thirteen.

What is evidently needed now is to set up pilot schools, perhaps schools of several different kinds, in different types of communities—in slum areas and rich suburbs, in company towns and scientific laboratory colonies—to try out this new personal and concrete and manipulative education in a streamlined program all the way from age one to age twenty-one or older. This may be the most exciting educational adventure of the next decade if we can find some educational leaders who will take the initiative in setting up private schools of this sort, or who can persuade some forward-looking school boards to try them out.

I think that if we put together all the speedups and simplifications that these new methods make possible, the children in such schools would no longer be overworked. The subjects we now teach them might be mastered in a much shorter school day, perhaps no more than three or four hours. There would be less boredom and resistance in school and more time for creative leisure outside. Some parents may shudder at this, because they do not want the children home half the day. But with the new trends of productivity and automation in our adult life, perhaps creative leisure is one of the things we need to teach earliest to children. And if we let the adult leisure enrich the children's leisure, homework might become home play and the interaction between the generations might make for better relations than we have had for years. The adults with all their new leisure in fact may now be going back to school, to learn in a more voluntary and serious way the subjects they missed in all their years of report-card education.

All this would change the pattern of education. The intense pattern we now impose across a few years in the late teens—where we have to study all day and all night because the earlier grades have taught us so little—might be replaced by an easier longitudinal pattern that would start with easy and fast learning methods at age one or two and would then go on all our lives for two or three or four hours a day. The children and the college students and the leisured adults might acquire a new attitude toward education. Formal teaching might blend inseparably into more individual and creative leisure-time activities, such as building boats together or learning music or ballet or skiing—or studying embryos and catching striped bass before dawn. Education would be by contagion and long discussion, and the generations might learn to talk to each other again.

A lifetime ago we made the transformation to education for living. It is time now to make the transformation to education for wholeness, for delight, and for diversity.

EDUCATION AND THE
CONTEMPORARY WOMAN

Anne Firor Scott

I can think of few more risky ways of spending an academic hour than discussing the education of women. Many gallons of ink, much breath, and maybe even a little blood are spent on this subject every year—without in the least promoting general agreement.

Yet it is a subject that I find impossible to avoid, as I examine the inadequacies of my own education, the hopes I have for a fifteen-year-old daughter, and the daily concerns of young women in my classes. In the process of examining this subject over the years, I have acquired a vast grab bag of ideas, bons mots, obiter dicta and the like, picked up from all kinds of people (mostly men) who write on the subject. What your invitation has forced me to do is to ask myself, Can I make any sense of all this talk? What do I myself really believe?

One means of making sense of any subject is to try to put it in some kind of order, and so my first step is to sort out the grab bag into three boxes: (1) How did we get here? In short, what do I know about the history of women's education? (2) What are the problems confronting women who seek to become educated today? and (3) What are some of the elements I would like to include in the education of young college women of this generation?

Women in any society or culture are always educated by the culture itself as to what the female role is. This is true in civilized societies as well as in primitive ones, but civilized societies are also concerned about whether women need formal education, and if so what its nature should be. Plato in the Fifth Book of the *Republic* finally decided that his female guardians would need the same education as the male guardians, even though he had some emotional doubts about this. Regardless of Plato's theory, however, we do not find any women taking part in the Socratic dialogue, which was the higher education of Plato's day.

Down the road a few kilometers from Athens, the Spartans had also given thought to the education of women and prescribed a very vigorous program, aimed at excellent physical development. This was primarily so that the women would have strong, healthy children—and if you follow the arguments about educating women through the ages you will frequently find that the central question is not, Does the woman need to be educated for her own benefit? but, Will it be good for the children?

In the Middle Ages most women were too hard at work even to learn to read, but a few great ladies were excellently taught; you may have heard of the *professoressa* at the University of Bologna who was so beautiful she had to wear a veil in order not to distract her students who were, presumably, mostly male. You have heard that Queen Elizabeth read Latin for pleasure (she said it was pleasure, anyway), and you may also know the remark in one of Defoe's essays: "A woman well bred and well taught is a creature without comparison. . . . She is all softness, and sweetness, peace, love, wit and delight. . . . Rob her of the benefits of education and . . . she degenerates to be turbulent, clamorous, noisy, nasty and the devil."

I am not sure that Defoe's opinion was shared in seventeenth-century Massachusetts where Mistress Anne Hutchinson used her formidable learning in theology to threaten the theocracy, or by Napoleon in the nineteenth century when he was so intimidated by the intellectual prowess of Madame de Staël that he ordered her not to come within forty miles of Paris. Madame de Staël's younger American contemporary Margaret Fuller calmly remarked: "I now know all the people worth knowing in America and I find no intellect comparable to my own." Which, as Perry Miller has commented, may have been the simple truth.

Few of these women, of course, had been to school. And they stand out because they are exceptional. Their experience tells us very little about the educational experience of everywoman. For that, let us rely for the moment only on American history.

In order to understand the history of education in this country, it is necessary to realize—and here I lean heavily on Bernard Bailyn's wonderful little book *Education in the Forming of American Society* (Chapel Hill: University of North Carolina Press, 1960)—what happened to the educational process when it was transferred to North America by the colonists. Bailyn cogently argues that it was in the American colonies that the process of separating education from the family—a process now far advanced in many parts of the world—began. Education became the pre-eminent means of adjusting to a rapidly changing world. It became the basis for social mobility and the road to power. Look at the Constitutional convention, for example, with its high proportion of college graduates.

Now what about women in all this? As long as education was a process of growing up in an extended family, in which fathers taught sons what they needed to know and mothers taught daughters, the women were as well educated for their role in life as the men. But in the colonies, with their wealth of free land, the extended family did not long survive. Parents' experience was no longer adequate to the needs of the new world: indeed, the children, being more malleable, might adjust better. And when schools outside the home flourished and colleges (such as Harvard, William and Mary, Kings, and Princeton) were founded for men only, what then?

The status of women had improved in America compared to England at the same time, but on this point able women had reason to feel aggrieved, and so they did. Read Abigail Adams' letters to John, deploring her lack of learning. Or note the wide sale of Mary Wollstonecraft's book in America.

If you add to the great importance that education assumed in the making of American society, the vast changes brought about by the Industrial Revolution, which gradually removed from the home many of the duties which had constituted woman's significant contribution to the economy and well-being of the family—in due course you get enough discontent to power the engine of change.

By the third decade of the nineteenth century, in conjunction with some men whose observation had convinced them that women cut off from what was becoming the mainstream of life did not make very good wives, a handful of women began to found colleges (as Mary Lyon at Mount Holyoke) or to attend colleges newly opened to women (as Lucy Stone at Oberlin). This was the beginning of a great revolution in the status of women in America.

Lest you think that it came easy, go back and read some of the bitter arguments of the time. Woman's physical structure could not stand the strain of study, it was said. They would get brain fever. And anyway their brains were too small. Above all, it was unladylike. Marion Talbot, who was the first dean of women at the University of Chicago, said that when she decided to go to college certain of her mother's friends never afterward spoke her name, and added that only in Washington "Women were kind to me for they did not know I was a college graduate."

And lest we grow too smug about how much was accomplished, it may be worth remembering that as late as the 1940 census only 3.7 per cent of the women over twenty-five in this country had had four years of college. Even today only 15 per cent of the young women in this country go to college.

Social change works in mysterious ways. The first generation of women college graduates were, intellectually speaking, "all dressed up and no place to go." They were educated (and had not died of brain fever) but the world did not welcome them as doctors, lawyers, college teachers, or in any of the hundreds of jobs in the business and professional world. One result was that many of them invented jobs for themselves—the most spectacular case in point taking place not many miles from here, on the corner of Polk and Halsted, where Jane Addams, who had gone to Rockford, and Julia Lathrop, who had been to Smith, Florence Kelley, a Cornell graduate, and Alice Hamilton, an early woman medical doctor, created at Hull House one of the most vital centers of social thought and action in America, and incidentally invented the profession of social work.

These and others like them created an alternative image for young American women.

Forty years earlier a girl had two possible destinies: if she was poor she might leave the farm and work in a factory where, with luck, she died young. If she stayed on the farm or if she was a member of the comfortable middle class, she grew up and got married, and if she failed in that goal she would be an old maid and live out her days as an unpaid servant in the house of some relative, the kind maiden aunt in all the stories, whom everybody imposed on because failures get imposed on.

By 1900—thanks to the bold pioneers—there was another alternative. You could grow up and go to college (if your father could be persuaded) and learn how to earn your own living, and then if the right man never came along you could stand on your own feet and even, if you had talent, carve out for yourself a significant place in the world. It is almost impossible for us today to comprehend what this meant to women who were not certain that the right man *would* come along, and who knew from firsthand experience how many miserable women there were, married to men they did not like or respect, and trapped with children they did not want (not in such numbers, anyway), because marriage was woman's only proper estate.

The first generation or two of women for whom education was available reveled in their freedom, to work, to travel, not to marry unless it suited them. But generations turn over quickly, and as college education for women became more common, the pioneering spirit began to dim. Girls found they might earn an A.B. and yet be married (Miss Thomas, the formidable president of Bryn Mawr, had once remarked— "Only our failures marry"—but that was in the early days when women's colleges were working so hard to be as intellectual as Harvard or Yale that they overshot the mark and became more intellectual than Harvard or Yale ever thought of being.)

Then another generation or two went by, and for reasons much discussed but by no means clear, there seems to have been a vast falling off in ambition. Girls still flock to college (all 15 per cent of them, that is), but among able high school graduates fewer women than men go on to college. Of those who do, some drop out before finishing, and it seems to be a problem if not a disgrace if one arrives at graduation without an engagement ring (a paradoxical inversion of Miss Thomas' celebrated comment.) Of women lawyers, the proportion remains about the same today as in 1910. Of women doctors the number remains small, and in the colleges and universities female professors are a small minority, becoming smaller. The women physicists in this country can hold a meeting in a hotel room, and the women economists do not require much more space. When President Johnson said in all sincerity (having counted the voters and finding women outnumbering men) that he wanted to appoint fifty women to high federal office not half that number could be found.

For nearly a decade discussion has swirled about this phenomenon, and though many theories have been advanced, no one has come up with a comprehensive explanation of the tides of fashion in women's role. Without knowing precisely why things are as they are, we can still ask what questions may be raised about women's education by this curious pattern of a revolution in reverse.

1. You will hear it said that some women are as capable as some men of doing any job, but that in this culture the subtle expectations of women's roles are such that girls grow up believing they are not capable of comprehending the really hard subjects or of doing the really hard jobs. This problem of expectation is to be identified all the way from kindergarten to graduate school, in overt and covert forms. Science and mathematics are the favorite examples of subjects that in some cultures girls flock to, but, which in ours are shunned. In the Moscow High School for example, 80 per cent of the college-bound women are said to be science majors.

2. You will hear it said that men are afraid of competition from women, and therefore—having got there first—bar the door. If this is a major problem we should not waste our time worrying about the education of women, but should forthwith embark upon the re-education of men. (This is not a joke, but may indeed be the heart of the matter.)

3. You will hear it said that society, since it really does not believe in achieving women, makes it as difficult as possible for women to marry and do something else in addition. Day care is only for the poor, household help is hard to get and inefficient. Children must be car-pooled where public transport is insufficient, and in any case need, or seem to need, large amounts of maternal supervision.

This is a perfectly enormous problem that cannot be tossed off lightly even in its relation to women's education. But it is a problem of the larger society.

If we come back to special questions of women in college, the arguments about curriculum and program planning for women students usually turn out to be based on one of three assumptions: (1) we should plan women's education according to their needs (usually unspecified, and rightly so, since no one knows for sure what they are); (2) we should plan women's education according to their capacities (which may or may not be the same as those of men, even if they are just as large); or (3) we should plan women's education according to the lives they are going to lead.

The trick would be to figure out a plan that would be based on all three of these assumptions. Is it possible?

1. As to needs, beyond food, shelter, and sex, I am not certain that any two psychologists have ever agreed on an inherent human need, much less one specific to women. Nevertheless, without being dogmatic perhaps one can say that most sensitive people feel a need to figure out what life is

all about. Part of what they want from college is help in making sense of their experience, in order to answer the questions What is it to be a man? What is it to be a woman? To male students we offer, as part of a liberal education, what men have thought on this question, from Plato to David Riesman.

To the extent that the question is a human question, a girl can learn a great deal by reading Aristotle or Locke or Rousseau. But in my ideal curriculum for women we will have also a seminar for freshman girls that will be based on reading what *women* have thought and felt about life, men, children, art, and religion—from Sappho to Margaret Mead. We would read the diaries and memoirs and letters and poems of women who were trying to make sense of their experience.

Beyond this, my ideal curriculum for women (as well as for men) would take each student in depth into at least one major area of knowledge so that by graduation the student would have a sense of mastery, of competence, which is the basis for self-respect. Such competence can have a subtle effect upon a woman's whole image of herself and a very pervasive influence upon her future life.

2. As to capacities, here I think the difference between men and women is insignificant. In each sex there are the truly remarkable, the very able, and the run-of-the-mill. All I ask for women is that the truly remarkable not find themselves rejected when they aspire, and that the very able and the run-of-the-mill have a chance to find out what options life holds beyond those they have experienced in their own families. This is as much a matter of faculty concern and attitudes as it is of curriculum.

3. As to educating women for the life they are going to lead, this is where some hard thinking needs to be done. It

is clear that a woman's life pattern, even if she elects to remain single, is going to be different from that of her contemporary men friends. If she marries, and if she has children, it will be very different.

I suspect the colleges should face up to this. I suspect that instead of commenting on all the difficulties and drawbacks that biology presents, we should ask ourselves how many of these could be turned into assets for women and for society. So, as I would offer the freshman girls a seminar on women through the ages, I would offer senior girls a seminar called "Where do you go from here?" I would encourage them to think, analyze, and shape their future plans to a program of on-going self-education. Much of women's daily life is concerned with direct experience, without the mediation of books, but this experience can be turned to account for educational purposes.

Most young women will leave the world of school and the world of work while their children are small. Does this mean stagnation, mental and physical? Not necessarily, but it does mean that planning and foresight are of the essence.

Obviously the ramifications of all these ideas are complex and would require the most careful thought. They are not parts of a tidy program, but an effort to reach out a bit from where we are and take hold of some visible problems.

PLATONIC EDUCATION

James M. Redfield

We are met here to consider the question, "What knowledge is most worth having?" or as I prefer to rephrase it, What is educational about education? I am going to talk today about some Platonic answers to this question. But a few prior warnings. In the first place I am not going to quote much from Plato or try to document my assertion that these answers are Platonic. Plato is hard to quote because he wrote not treatises but dialogues; he does not talk about education so much as he exhibits it. In any case, I have not composed a piece about Plato; I have composed a piece about education, starting from the picture Plato gives us of Socrates the educator. So I have not concerned myself with the question of whether the statements I make represent the views of Plato or of Redfield; it is enough if they are something like true statements.

In the second place, when I speak of education I limit it to that which can be learned from speech and writing and which can be expressed in symbols, verbal or otherwise. I exclude from my sphere of reference the school of hard knocks, mystical revelation, and all other educational modes whose teachings cannot be expressed in language.

In the third place, I begin from the assumption that the aim of education, like the aim of every other human activity, is happiness. Of course I am assuming a mere tautology, but even a tautology can serve to direct our attention. I think we should be asking, not what knowledge is reputable or exciting, but what knowledge is good for us. And since I am talking about statable knowledge my question is really, in the phrase of Hans Jonas, What are the practical uses of theory?

The question, "What knowledge is most worth having?" is dependent on a prior question: What knowledge is there? In the *Apology* Socrates tells us that he went looking for knowledgeable men. He went first to the statesmen and the poets, and he found that neither class knew anything; the statesmen worked from certain rules of thumb and the poets by divine inspiration. Neither class could explain what it did. Then he went to the craftsmen and found that they do in fact know "many and wonderful things." The craftsman does in fact possess knowledge; he can do things other men cannot; he can tell us how he does them; he can point to his teacher and he can teach others. So when Plato talks about knowledge he always begins with the crafts.

Each craft, furthermore, is a kind of knowledge worth having, insofar as it meets human need and human wishes. We require craft because nature is recalcitrant to our will. We cannot simply do what we decide to do; we must also know how to do it. We cannot acquire a table simply by choosing to have it; nor is it enough to have set aside the time and energy, the tools and materials required for tablemaking; we must also know how to make a table. We must come to terms with nature so that we can act according to nature's laws; if we possess no craft we will conclude our activity, not with a table, but with a heap of scraps and sawdust.

We do not ascribe knowledge to the craftsman, further, simply because he has a capacity for a given activity; a craft is not simply the capacity for shaping matter into form. If such a capacity were called knowledge we would have to ascribe knowledge to the nest-building bird and the web-making spider. Socrates went about asking, not for demonstrations, but for explanations. The statesmen and the poets can act, but they cannot explain their actions. The craftsmen, on the other hand, can explain, and they can teach others how to imitate them. In the Socratic phrase, their opinion is "accompanied by discourse."

The tradition of a craft, then, has two parts, practice and theory, skill and method. The skill of a craftsman is in the hand, like the instinctive behavior of the animals, but his method is proved in the specifically human mode of speech. Skill is a mode of doing, but method is a mode of knowing. The palsied carpenter is a carpenter no longer but he still possesses the method of carpentry; he cannot build a table but he can tell us how to build one. On the other hand, a man might have acquired the knack of building a table without ever learning the method of carpentry; his tables are satisfactory but he cannot teach us to make them. Probably, also, he does not know the limits of his knowledge until he tries to explain to us what he does. Skill is maintained by practice, but method is maintained by teaching.

So the crafts give us one model for education. We might take education to be the teaching of those methods which are likely to be useful to us. Furthermore, every activity is accompanied by some method; there are methods of practice and methods of theory; history and metaphysics have their methods, and so does ethics, and even poetry and statesmanship have some methodological statements to make—even though, the more serious the activity, the less adequately the method seems to explain it. Presumably we cannot create poets and statesmen, but we can teach our students what there is to know about these activities, and then, with whatever misgivings, leave them on their own.

But in this case education will not be adequate to happiness. In the first place, we do not know what methods are likely to be useful to us. Life is a chapter of accidents, and use is relative to the needs of the moment. Ten yards from a lifeboat in mid-Atlantic we may find ourselves saying, "If only

I had learned to swim," but such possibilities do not give swimming a necessary place in education.

In the second place, we usually do not know what our needs are, which is to say, we do not know what would make us happy. Should I try to make more money? Or do a job that interests me? Should I try to secure more time to myself? Or should I take on more students? Each of these choices can make a case for itself, and I won't know which is most rewarding until I try; once I have tried it will be too late to try something else. Only at moments of crisis, floundering around the lifeboat, do our needs seem clear to us. That is the attractive thing about crisis: it tells you what knowledge is most worth having and so reduces the problem of knowledge to a technical problem. I have heard it suggested that the knowledge most worth having is the knowledge which would produce world peace, but while I am sure that a reasonable state of peace is necessary to happiness, I also know that it is not sufficient. And I do not know what else will be needed.

Man, in other words, is mortal. He is vulnerable, first, to circumstance, and since he cannot predict his circumstances, he cannot confidently equip himself to meet them. Second, in a limited life he must decide to do some things and not others, and so must decide to learn some things and not others. If we, like the Homeric gods, were immortal, we could learn all possibly useful methods and undertake all the activities for which they prepared us; over an infinite period of time we could perhaps come to happiness. As it is we must, in education as in everything else, make our best guess and launch ourselves into the void.

So far, however, I have only shown that the problem of education is insoluble, not that it is difficult. We are accustomed to coming to terms with our mortality; we make our choices within a known frame of ignorance. Even the carpenter does not know when he will strike a knot; nor does he know whether next year's customers will be asking for tables or for chairs. He studies his material as best he can, he makes his best guess at the future state of the market, and he equips himself accordingly.

Since carpentry is the art of transforming wood so that it meets human demand, the carpenter can tell whether or not his work is successful. If his products are demanded he is working well; if they are not he fails. So far I have been talking about happiness in the same terms, as though we could know whether or not we are happy. Socrates also sometimes makes this assumption, as in the *Protagoras* when he says that if happiness consisted in the greatest amount of pleasure and the least amount of pain, the knowledge most worth having would be that method which enabled us to predict, to the highest degree of human accuracy, the pleasures and pains resulting from our choices.

But Socrates knows that his assumption is fallacious, and from him I have learned so too. Happiness is incorrigibly plural. How shall I pass the evening? Shall I make a snowman? Read a more or less elevating book? Write a memorandum? Play with my child? Drink? I find all these activities rewarding, and their rewards are incommensurate. I have no common scale of delight for the comparative measurement of politics, theory, play, art, and self-indulgence. All of these things are good; I know *that* because I am sure that a life in which they all appear is better than a life from which any one is excluded. For the same reason I know that one is not better than another; if politics were better than art I would want as much politics as possible and as little art, or vice versa. The best life seems to me a life in which all these things have their proper place, and determining what is good about any one of them will not enable me to determine the proper balance between them. Yet, since the soul is bound by space, time, and its own singularity, I must at every moment make some judgment of proportion among all the good things that I see.

Method, therefore, can contribute to happiness, but there can be no method of happiness. Methods tell us how to achieve some stated good; the good is relative to the method. For the doctor *qua* doctor the good sought is health; the doctor's method enables him to have his best shot at healing his patients. But the art of medicine cannot tell him whether to visit three querulous old ladies or go home to dinner. He must make that decision for himself.

This, I think, is what Socrates means when he says that the knowledge most worth having is the knowledge of the Good,

> . . . that which every soul pursues and for the sake of which it does everything, making a prophetic guess that it is something, but uncertain and unable to take proper hold of it, nor to reach any permanent position about it as we can in the case of other things—and for this reason the soul fails to make proper use even of those other things that are useful . . . (*Republic* 505d,e)

> This, the idea of the Good, . . . is the highest knowledge; as we act according to it we make justice and everything else useful and beneficial. I suppose you also know . . . that we do not adequately know it. But if we do not know it, even if we should know everything else to the greatest degree of perfection, they are no help to us, just as if we should possess something and that thing should not be good. You don't think that we get anywhere by owning any possession if it is not in fact good? Or by having every form of intelligence without intelligence of the good, so that our intelligence is not related to the human good?
> Good lord no, he said. (*Republic* 505a,b)

The Good is unlike other objects of knowledge in that it is both infinitely close to us and infinitely distant, perfectly immanent and perfectly transcendent. Each choice we make is a declaration of our judgment of the best thing for us as we are at that moment and in those circumstances; in this sense the good is infinitely various. Yet each choice is also a commitment of the whole self, a declaration that, starting from where we are, this step takes us one step closer to happiness.

Furthermore we are to some extent what we choose to be; so every choice is a choice of something and also a choice of self. The man who decides to make a table also decides to be a carpenter; the man who sets out to classify plants is guided by an idea of himself as a knower; the man who sets out to remedy an injustice is guided by an idea of himself as a charitable being. Since the process of self-creation is indefinitely extensible, we are always guided, in choice, by a sense, however inchoate, of the perfection of man.

So Socrates sometimes talks about knowledge of the Good and sometimes about knowledge of the self. Nor are these two kinds of knowledge different. As we reflect upon our choices, as we make their real character clear to ourselves, our activity becomes more fully rational and thus more fully human. We come to be what we in fact are. He encourages us to know ourselves not as we happen to have become, but as we are capable of being.

It is also clear that prior to the choice of self is the choice to *be* a self. Implicit in our choosing activity is an assertion that we want to make ourselves and not be made by others. Man is distinguished from an animal or an instrument by his capacity for considered choice; our capacity for deliberation keeps us from being a mere part of the machine of nature.

Our awareness of our freedom is the foundation of our sense of our own identity. Autonomy, therefore, is the necessary condition of happiness, and the man who has achieved autonomy, who takes responsibility for himself, while he cannot be said to have *achieved* happiness, can be said to *really pursue* it.

For Plato, then, the aim of education is to bring man, not to happiness, but to the pursuit of happiness. So far it should be clear that Plato, to his credit, agrees with Wayne Booth. And it should be clear that there is nothing educational about method. The essence of method is repetition. Practical method is the knowledge of how to predict and control nature; the craftsman or scientist tells us that if we do X, Y will result; he knows this because he and his fellows have done X countless times and Y has usually occurred. Theoretical method is, in Aristotle's phrase, "a capacity for demonstration," it provides us with the capacity to prove to ourselves or to another the truth of what we already know. The knowledge of method gives you a capacity to repeat yourself, and when you teach method you teach others to repeat after you. Method is memory systematized into statement.

But choice is never repetitious. Choice is free because each choice is a new determination of the best. Insofar as a man repeats himself he becomes like an animal or a machine. The potter who transforms on his wheel lump after lump of clay into an endless row of identical jars does not choose to make each jar like the others; at most he chooses not to choose, letting his mind wander as his hands work. He is an excellent potter, he has mastered his method, but he is not choosing or judging; for the sake of the jars he has given up some of his humanity. So also the historian, if any there be, who applies the same method to one archive after another. To sit at the feet of the master craftsman and learn his method as he teaches it is to turn from the pursuit of happiness toward the loss of self.

What kind of education, then, contributes to the achievement of autonomy? In answering this question Socrates makes a few observations upon the human situation. In the first place, while it is good to satisfy our desires, happiness does not consist in the satisfaction of desire. My desires do not bear thinking on; I don't need Sigmund Freud to tell me that. At the core of every man is Plato's tyrant, devoted to the desires which, as Socrates says, appear in most men "only in dreams." Let me loose and I would turn to rape, cannibalism, incest. The energy at the core of every man is idle, self-destructive passion, primitive, inchoate, and therefore insatiable. We cannot find our principle of action in that which is itself perfectly unprincipled.

Man is a part of nature; he lives in contact with an environment, he occupies a body, and his soul also has a nature. "Of soul too there is a physics," says Aristotle, "insofar as it partakes of the material." But the Socratic self-knowledge is not the physics of soul; he does not mean that we pursue happiness by learning that "this is the sort of thing that always makes me angry" or "I'll bet I'll get a boot out of that." Our impulses are part of our situation, as the conditions of our choice. But to choose is to be free of our situation; therefore the pursuit of happiness begins from the denial of impulse.

The beginning of education, then, is temperance. But not such temperance as the world knows. We do not become autonomous by being good little boys and girls, but because we have caught sight of something more interesting than pleasure. Socrates recommends all the social virtues—temperance, courage, wisdom, and justice—but he does not recommend them for the reasons given by society.

Society is the method that men have corporately evolved for coexisting with nature. This coexistence has two parts. We have learned to live with our natural environment; we have invented techniques for controlling and shaping it to our comfort and safety. And we have learned also to live with the nature of man, to shape that also to our comfort and safety. To this end we have invented morality. Morality, says Socrates, is the controlled gratification of impulse. Society promises us some pleasures on condition that we abstain from others; if we break the rules society will punish us and see that our pleasures are turned to pains. The pleasures that are socially acceptable, on the other hand, are doubly rewarding; they please in themselves and they bring with them the assistance and approval of our neighbors.

Society is the grand method that validates all the others. Every activity aims at some good; every methodical activity works rationally toward some good; society rationalizes the whole pattern of our activities by telling us what particular goods are worth pursuing. In this social order technique and morality overlap; in any society that which is useful is also accounted honorable.

It is according to the standard of society that all methods are recommended to us. The potter works because there is a market for his pots; in the same way we tell our students that if they will learn the method of philosophy there will be open to them a well-paid and reputable profession. Society tells us, from its own point of view, what knowledge is most worth having; that point of view asserts that the aim of education is socialization. General education thus provides men with that knowledge which, as members of a single community, they all require, while special education fits them to make some special contribution to the common good.

Of course education, like every other human activity, cannot happen except within the social order. Because education requires the support of society, those institutions whose declared purpose is educational are rightly expected to help society operate. But, says Socrates, socialization is not in itself educational. Society as a mode of human existence bears against autonomy; if the social order were perfected we would all be reduced to the level of the bee or the ant. Society decides for us; we pursue happiness by learning to decide for ourselves. Therefore education always begins from the rejection of social tradition.

The foundation of the Socratic education, therefore, is the *elenchus,* the process of refutation by which the student is convinced that he does not know what he thought he knew, that he cannot defend whatever received opinions he carries about with him. In itself the *elenchus* is a sophistical exercise; Socrates will use any means—fair or foul—to convince the student of his inadequacy. The aim of the *elenchus* is not to impart truth or even to convict error; it aims to show the student that he cannot defend himself with the weapons society has given him and suggests to him the necessity of learning to defend himself.

The *elenchus* is a dangerous process; Socrates often compares it to major surgery. Society has come to terms with the chaos of impulse by imposing on it an ordered routine of practice and opinion. Since society and impulse are in conflict they often come to seem alternative; we feel that we must choose between passion and duty. By cracking the structure of the student's habitual opinions Socrates is making an opening, it seems, for anarchy; if society's prohibitions are invalid, then perhaps everything is permitted.

Socrates meets this problem by simultaneously separating the student from his peers and involving him with the teacher. The *elenchus* is at once a shock and an invitation; "You do not know how to talk," says Socrates; "I have proved that. But at the same time I have shown that I, who assert that I know nothing, know more about talking than you do. Stay and talk with me, and perhaps you can learn it too." The Socratic *elenchus* makes the student helpless, and at the same time it makes him dependent on Socrates. By means of the *elenchus* Socrates recruits members for the Socratic circle, the group of young men who follow Socrates and answer his questions.

The Socratic circle is a subsociety with its own social norms. So there is another danger to the *elenchus:* it can free the student only to subject him to a new mode of social rigor— the more limiting in that the philosophical society is smaller and more compact. The teacher's task is to make this sub- society which he directs the arena of autonomy rather than conformity. The Socratic teacher must take care that his teaching does not degenerate into just another method. If he makes his students his disciples he has become a sophist, and has failed.

The Socratic dialogues tell us relatively little about the teacher's strategies for attaining this end. Most of the dia- logues represent Socrates in battle with his sophistic com- petitors or recruiting the young for his own circle. Only two dialogues, the *Republic* and the *Phaedo,* take place within the Socratic circle, and they do not show us the whole pattern of Socratic education; they are at best representative samples, brief excerpts from a continuing conversation.

One thing, however, we can say. There are current in the Socratic circle, as Plato represents it, certain doctrines. These doctrines shift a bit from dialogue to dialogue but funda- mentally Socrates is consistent about them. He tells his stu- dents that the soul is immortal, that they have lived before, that they will be judged after death, that the soul has three parts, and so on. These doctrines are never proved or defended; they are simply introduced into argument when they become necessary. Nevertheless they play an important role in the Socratic conversation, and by considering them we might learn something about the educational character of those conversations. Here I address myself to only one doctrine, perhaps the most important: the so-called Theory of Ideas.

The Theory of Ideas asserts that there are two worlds, one composed of the objects of perception, multiple, material, and mutable, the other of the objects of knowledge, simple, immaterial, and eternal. There are trees and there is Tree. By this doctrine Socrates points to a commonplace fact about our experience: that the intellect lives in a world not of things but of concepts. So long as we have no name for a tree, so long as we do not place it in any general category, we really have no experience of it at all; it remains for us a blob of inchoate perceptions. Before we can pay our tree *any* humane attention we must notice that it *is* something, that it is, for instance, a tree. So in a sense there is *no* knowledge of the particular: all knowledge is of the universal.

Socrates, however, goes further; he talks of the particular and the universal as separate objects of knowledge, and asserts that we know the particular by comparing it with the universal. Socrates talks about the ideas as if they were things; he has taken a fact about knowing and treated it as a fact about being. By so doing he falls into a set of logical absurdities, ably set forth by Plato himself in the first part of the *Parmenides,* and expanded by Plato's adversaries ever since.

Not content with this, Socrates asserts that the ideas are the realest things, and that the objects of our experience are merely their imitations. The trees we meet are more or less imperfect pictures of Tree; the plural trees have the sort of diminished reality that all imitations have. The experienced tree is really experienced but it is not really Tree, just as a picture of George is really a picture but it is not really George.

According to Socrates, however, those imitative things are the only things we *do* experience—at least in this life. In another life, he says, we saw the ideas themselves—but now we have forgotten them; we remember them only to the degree that things here are capable of reminding us of the original. We look at the picture and say, "that's George," but we are in the position of a man who knows George only through his pictures and who never has an opportunity to check the picture against the original.

The Theory of Ideas is thus a troubling way of talking about knowledge. Since an imitation is by definition imperfect—otherwise it would be a re-creation—the knowledge that we have got is by nature the knowledge least worth having. And the knowledge most worth having is, according to Socrates, knowledge that we cannot acquire.

Here let us remember that according to the Simile of Light in the *Republic* the Good is both the source of the intelligibility of the other ideas and the source of their existence. That is, the true locus of knowledge is not contemplation but rather choice. And when we are choosing we are not concerned with what is but what should be; therefore precisely that which is *not* in the field of our experience is the focus of our attention. The nurseryman, for example, is concerned only secondarily with his trees as they are, primarily with his trees as they should be. His aim is to produce the best tree, that is, he has his eye on Tree. He works with his trees precisely when they diverge from the Tree he has in his mind. Therefore we can say, without departing from common sense, that the trees he sees are imperfect imitations of the Tree he has never seen.

The Theory of Ideas, in fact, describes the world as it is encountered by the practical intelligence.

A man acting for a purpose is always, in Diotima's phrase, between Poverty and Resource. He must find his present situation unsatisfactory; otherwise he would sit still. He must see some prospect of improvement; otherwise he would have no place to go. Out of his present need he generates an idea of future improvement; this idea sharpens his sense of Poverty and leads him to action. As he begins to act upon the world, to realize his idea, his experience sharpens his idea and deepens his sense of Resource. Thus thought leads to action and action in turn leads to thought. Nor is the Resource at any stage something exterior to the situation of the actor; the Resource is the Poverty itself formulated, so that we feel our situation, not simply as lack, but as lack of something.

The clearest instance, I think, is the case of invention. Consider a man drinking water from his hands. The water trickles through his fingers, he cannot drink without getting his face wet, he cannot in this way carry water more than a few feet. Such a man, if he is gifted, may out of his discomforts conceive the notion of a cup. To begin with the cup is for him simply something that his hands are not. As he pursues his notion, as he shapes clay, metal, and even plastic to his purpose, he refines his idea; every cup he makes is both a cup and not *yet* a cup. Each invention is a partial success, but it does not yet satisfy its inventor; each new dissatisfaction, as it becomes explicit to the cup-maker, suggests a better cup. So, in Socratic language, the process of invention is a progressive imitation of Cup.

In one sense the idea of a cup is an idea of the world, a world so transformed as to include cups. But in another sense it is an idea of self: the idea that a man could be a cup-maker and a cup-user. The cup will not be made until it has been both conceived and chosen; we must come to think both that cups are possible and that they are desirable. Therefore the invention of the cup implies that the cup-using man is a better sort of man than the cupless. Seen this way our sense of Poverty is a sense of our own imperfection; our sense of Resource a sense of what we could be.

Invention, in fact, is one of the modes of autonomy. The inventor of the cup, at the moment when he first takes the clay in his hand and begins to shape it, is free; the mark of his freedom is that he is both selfless and self-absorbed; he is neither methodical nor impulsive. There is nothing self-indulgent in his activity; he moves straight toward the human good as he sees it. Nor is he taking direction from anyone; his act, to the degree that it is creative, is entirely his own. So also the poet as the words form into music in his mind, and the statesman as he collects his resources for the reform of society. All of their products, when they succeed, become part of the cultivated routine, but the originators, as they shape society, are also free of it.

Creativity is occasional because it is unmethodical and therefore unrepeatable. We create precisely when we do not know what we are doing; we know our creative acts only in doing them. The poet knows how to write his poems; the proof is that he has written them. But he does not know how to write poems; having written some he is never sure he can write more. He cannot explain his method; if he can explain it he is not a creative poet. Creativity is the discovery of self in activity; it is therefore personal and incommunicable.

And yet we do not feel the creative experience as one of confusion. When we decide, in spite of the exhaustion of our energies and the doubts of our friends, that honor compels us to an unpopular and unpleasant act, we reach a state of moral certainty; our behavior, however eccentric, is not erratic. We are sure that we know what we are doing, even though we cannot explain it. Such moments are rare in any life, but memorable, and they are moments of lucidity. At these moments we best know ourselves engaged in the active pursuit of happiness.

By the Theory of Ideas Socrates asserts that the creator does not act blindly. He has his eye on something, though not on anything at present in the world of his experience. By describing the ends of action as objects of knowledge, Socrates asserts that freedom is action in a direction, that creativity is more than idle restless trial and error. Man, he says, does not blunder into autonomy; he *claims* his freedom from method and impulse because he has caught sight of something more persuasive to his act than either.

The Theory of Ideas thus describes a world in which autonomy is possible. And since autonomy is identity we all assent to that Theory insofar as we attempt at all to make our lives our own. The Theory does not have to be proved; it is simply a statement of the world in which as pursuers of happiness we all live.

Notice that the Theory of Ideas never appears at the beginning of a Socratic dialogue. It appears always in the middle, as a familiar doctrine now again appropriate. The relevance of the Theory of Ideas, in fact, is the test of the seriousness of any discourse. When that Theory becomes an appropriate element of our talk we are talking about the pursuit of happiness and can entertain some proper hope that our talk is educational.

The Theory of Ideas, however, is not in itself educational; at most it makes explicit the aims of education. Education, says Socrates, is the exercise of the soul; it occurs not by the comprehension of propositions but by the development of capacities. Therefore the Socratic student does not learn the

Socratic doctrine; he becomes involved with those doctrines as a part of his involvement with the Socratic discourse. And this involvement develops in him the capacity for freedom.

But here we have a problem, for the Socratic conversations are not deliberative but theoretical. Socrates does not ask, What shall we do now? He asks, What is justice? He does not ask, How are you and I to get on together? He asks, What is friendship? The Socratic students do not practice virtue; they talk about it. So the dialogues raise in radical form the question of the proper use of theory.

Theory can be *seen* to be useful when it leads to an ordered routine of practice, when the theory is a method. Socrates often talks about his own discourse in this way. He talks as if we could come to know the Ideas through talk and then use this knowledge in action. When we have decided what justice is, he says, we will know why we should be just; when we have decided what friendship is we will be friends. But this is absurd. The Ideas are not hypotheses but objects of choice; we never work from them, only toward them. Socrates proposes to us a contradiction in terms: methodical creativity.

The man of true virtue, says Socrates, would pursue happiness with the same quiet confidence with which the craftsman approaches his work. The horsebreaker knows horses, says Socrates; therefore he can improve them; let us know ourselves and we will be able to improve ourselves. The carpenter knows tables; therefore he approaches his workbench with a serene hope of success. Let us know the Good and we will approach the human situation with the same serene hope.

But we cannot approach the human situation; we are in it wherever we are. If we try to determine in advance the criteria of choice, that activity of determining the criteria must in itself correspond to the criteria. The quest for theoretical knowledge of the act does not take you toward the act but away from it. Every explanation requires a further explanation. The philosopher seeks not only to know how to act but to know that he knows, but how can he know whether or not he knows that he knows?

The answer, of course, is that he cannot. In fact the one thing he knows is that he is never sure. Hence the well-known Socratic ignorance; Socrates' knowledge begins, and in a sense ends, with a knowledge of the limits of human knowledge.

What escape can there be from this regress? Here let us go back a step and observe that method is free from the regress only because it is instrumental, because it is theory in the service of some externally defined good. We are involved in the regress, however, whenever we attempt to define the good, to validate those things that are valued for themselves. So far I have talked only of practical autonomy, but the same problem arises in the sphere of pure theory, of knowledge pursued for its own sake. "All men by nature desire to know," says Aristotle; knowledge is one of the modes of happiness. And happiness is no more obtainable here than in any other mode.

Some historian, let us say, fired with curiosity about a given time and place, attacks the relevant documents. As he works he makes progress; certain truths can in fact be discovered by careful interpretation of the evidence. But the more he learns the more he comes to be aware of his ignorance. History is a tissue of lacunae; between any two facts the historian knows there exist an indefinite number of facts he does not know. One causal explanation always requires another: perhaps a social change caused a political change, but what caused the social change? No piece of history is self-contained; the better the historian knows one period, the more aware he is of the need for examining its sources, parallels, and results. Because the part has meaning only in relation to the whole the historian cannot be confident even of the knowledge he has obtained. He may completely misinterpret the things he knows because he does not connect them with the things he does not know. Around any area of knowledge there is a perimeter of ignorance; as the area expands the perimeter expands also. The more the knower prepares himself to make adequate statements the more aware he becomes of the inadequacy of any statement he can make.

Yet this difficulty does not cripple historians. The historian does not expect to perfect his knowledge. He goes on until he feels ready to make a statement about what he's doing, to offer a lecture, an essay, a book. Each statement is a rough draft, an attempt to show the reader how far he has come. The reader is impressed by his learning; he himself is impressed by his ignorance. Yet because he can say something of interest to others his inquiry comes to something; it does not come to knowledge, but it comes to discourse.

That is the paradox of theory; it cannot be known but it can be taught. The theoretician does not, of course, teach definitive truth; that would be sophistry. He shows the work he has done; he explains to the reader where he is and enables the reader to come as far as he has come. *We* do not make progress by knowing what we know, but others can make progress by coming to know what we know. So our knowledge is not satisfactory to us, but it is, as they learn it, satisfactory to them.

As the pupil masters the learning of the teacher he becomes caught up in the same process; the more he learns from us the more he becomes aware of what we have not taught him. As he attempts to fill these gaps he ceases to be a student and becomes an inquirer; as his inquiry gives rise to statement he becomes a teacher. So we are not teaching him history; we are teaching him to be an original teacher of history. And to be an original teacher is the greatest happiness of the theoretician.

Inquiry, thus, makes possible discourse, and discourse inquiry. Many such inquirers, living in a community, constitute an intellectual tradition. If we ask what each inquirer seeks, we must answer that he seeks to know, but if we ask what he achieves, we must answer that he keeps the intellectual tradition alive. Discourse is not about nothing; on the contrary it is about truth. It can never be adequate to truth, however; it can only be adequate to further discourse. Through inquiry and statement the theoretician, as he seeks truth, establishes his relation to, and his independence of, the community of his peers.

Disputation is the mode of commonality of the community of discourse; alone among human communities this one thrives on disagreement. The community of discourse, therefore, is the proper home of the autonomous man. In this republic each citizen discovers himself in the other as each separately pursues the common and transcendent good.

The Socratic circle was such a community of discourse—dominated by a great teacher whose students in their turn became extraordinarily diverse teachers. Ignorant and questioning, Socrates pursued with his students his inquiry into the human situation and drew them into freedom. Wherever you are, he taught them, you can consider where you are and attempt to explain your situation. The pursuit of happiness cannot be founded on knowledge, but it can be activity "accompanied by discourse."

From his experience of the Socratic circle, Plato created the Academy and so founded the tradition of the universities. That tradition we still have with us. And we still have with us Plato's Socratic dialogues to remind us that no question is worth asking unless it raises, explicitly or implicitly, the question, "What knowledge is most worth having?"

THE BATTLE OF THE BOOKS

Richard McKeon

If the question set for us had been, "What knowledge is worth having?" the answer would have been, "All knowledge." But if that answer were given, we should have become involved in equivocations concerning what constitutes knowledge, and (if it is worth having by definition) by whom it is thought to be worth having (the demand for knowledge is exceeded by many other demands on the open market), and for what purpose it is thought to be worth having (the answer "for its own sake" might seem to depend on circularity in argument). Still more equivocations arise in discussing the question, "What knowledge is most worth having?"—equivocations concerning the order of acquiring knowledge, the manner of discovering it, the means of imparting and disseminating it, and, finally, the supreme equivocation of our times, the comforting anxiety that for the first time in history no one man could survey the accumulations of knowledge in all fields as the virtuosi of the Renaissance and the eighteenth century were still able to master all knowledge. It is important to understand, before undertaking the discussion of education, why that discussion, like any other fundamental discussion, is involved in equivocation. To achieve such understanding, however, it is necessary to avoid becoming involved in the total equivocation that is frequently the mark of a fundamental discussion. I have therefore chosen to discuss what knowledge is most worth having in terms of a single equivocation, one of the most persistent and inclusive of controversies, the battle of the books, or the quarrel of the ancients and the moderns.

The title is borrowed from Swift's *An Account of a Battel*

between the Ancient and Modern Books in St. James Library,
published in 1704 together with *A Tale of a Tub.* They were
written in defense of Swift's patron, Sir William Temple, who
had published *An Essay upon the Ancient and Modern
Learning* in 1690. The very considerable amount of scholarship that has been devoted to the quarrel makes it difficult
to understand. There had been a similar quarrel between the
ancients and the moderns in France, but again there is little
scholarly agreement about the influence of the one on the
other. If it is true that the battle of the books still goes on and
that the discussion of liberal education and general education
are skirmishes in it, the determination of what knowledge is
most worth having shares with other phases of the battle both
a tendency to ask questions which run into quibbles, con-
futations, and satirizations and yet to raise issues which determine major stages in the evolution of education and culture.
The questions seem trivial because of their basic and far-
reaching ambiguity; the issues are major because they affect
our conception of art, science, and practice and our use of
them in the development of character and communication.
In both respects, the battle of the books at the turn of the
seventeenth and eighteenth centuries may serve as an introduction to the knowledge most worth having.

The ambiguities of the battle of the books are of three sorts:
an ambiguity about the arts and the sciences, an ambiguity
about the relation of the arts and sciences to religion and
politics, and an ambiguity about the old and the new in the
knowledge most worth having. The first ambiguity has led to
the supposition that the quarrel was between ancient and
modern philosophy and science and only secondarily about
literature in England, whereas it was between ancient and
modern literature and only secondarily about philosophy and
science in France. All the important words, like "discipline,"

"art," and "science," are ambiguous precisely because what they stand for was in process of growth and transformation. To treat them as if they had a single meaning is to make the discussion a series of absurdities. When we talk about the interrelations of the "disciplines" today, we think of the disciplines as subject matters and bodies of knowledge. Late medieval, Renaissance, and early modern battles of the books marked the transition from disciplines conceived as arts and methods to disciplines conceived as fields and established bodies of knowledge. The sciences borrowed from the humanities in the late Middle Ages and the Renaissance: the first formulations of scientific method were derived from rhetoric, dialectic, and sophistic; philosophy and the humanities had begun to seek a scientific method in the seventeenth and eighteenth centuries: the Newtonian and Cartesian methods were used to form sciences of human nature, morals, and criticism. The Renaissance revolt against Aristotle made use of other ancient philosophers, like Plato and Democritus; the eighteenth-century revolt against Aristotle made use of modern philosophers like Bacon, Descartes, and Locke.

The second ambiguity arises from the relation of the arts and the sciences to values and society, to religion and politics. When the use of reason and of arguments is considered, instances or problems are usually sought in science and literature. Yet the problems of the interrelations among the disciplines are determined by and include the relations of the disciplines to actions and to values. The disciplines are actions and affect values. Swift states the reason for the extension satirically in the opening sentence of the Preface to *A Tale of a Tub*: the Wits of the present are so very numerous and penetrating that the Grandees of Church and State begin to fall under horrible Apprehensions lest they pick holes in the weak sides of Religion and Government. The problem of education is the problem of the relation of reason and argument to society and religion as well as to morals, arts, and sciences; it is the problem of the relation of reason and argument to social values and ultimate realities.

The third and fundamental ambiguity in a battle of changing fronts and of regrouping contestants is in the identity of the opponents, that is, the recognition of the ancients and the moderns, the determination of what is established and what is new. It is not a simple question to be answered by calling classical scholars ancients and contemporary satirists moderns. Swift was an ancient; his opponent, Richard Bentley, the modern, was a great classical scholar, one of the innovators of modern methods of studying the classics. The use of "modern" philological and scholarly methods often made "ancient" methods of interpreting texts irrelevant and understanding them unnecessary, as when Bentley undermined Sir William Temple's judgment and commendation of the letters of Phalaris and the fables of Aesop by showing them to be inauthentic. Bentley gave no interpretation of what the texts said once he had shown them to be spurious, in spite of the fact that apocryphal works have been important and influential and that our interpretation of Aristotle is still influenced by the works of pseudo-Aristotle and the commentaries of the pseudo-Aristotelians as well as by the works of Aristotle. Dr. Bentley was Royal Librarian of St. James Library, in which the Battle of the Books took place.

The ambiguity concerning the ancients and the moderns is not removed by placing the battles of the seventeenth and eighteenth centuries in the sequence of other quarrels of ancients and moderns: in the Renaissance, the "moderns," who affected Greek and called themselves "neoterics," cultivated the arts that Peter Ramus had instituted to repair the imperfections of the ancient and medieval liberal arts; in the fourteenth century, the *"antiqui"* and the *"moderni"* were logicians who battled about the principles and methods of one of the liberal arts; in ancient Rome, where the liberal arts were enumerated and described, the quarrels were political and social: one could not be a "modern," since *"modernus"* is a postclassical word, but one might take pride in being a *"homo novus,"* that is, the first of one's family to hold high office (and therefore—favorable or pejorative—a man newly ennobled or an upstart). Cato the Censor, who was a staunch opponent of Greek learning as a danger to native Roman virtues and who was said to have been taught Greek in his old age by the poet Ennius, was a *homo novus* and the remains of his writings are the beginning of Latin prose literature. When they are placed in the series of changing circumstances and applications, the battles of the ancients and the moderns seem puzzling and pointless, and to have no significant relation to each other or to the circumstances and problems of their times. Neither the ancients nor the moderns won at any stage in the two thousand years of war; or, more accurately, since there is so little agreement concerning what they were fighting about, both sides won and both lost. The battles of the books could easily be ignored, except for literary diversion or literary scholarship, if the battle were not still raging and if the arguments did not state problems of profound importance in terms that still waver on the edge of nonsense.

The battles of the ancients and the moderns mark the major stages in the development of Western Education and (what is the same thing) Western Culture and Learning; and the significance of the battles for the onward march can be seen by placing them in the context of the methods of the liberal arts and the problems of the arts and sciences on which they were practiced. The battle of the *antiqui* and the *moderni* in the fourteenth and the fifteenth centuries was a battle of logic. It was based on the newly translated works of Aristotle. The translation of Aristotle in the twelfth and thirteenth centuries was an event of overwhelming importance, since it made available in one block a new method of inquiry and proof and a body of sciences and scientific problems treated according to that method. It was a quarrel concerning the problems and the principles of the sciences. Humanistic studies were concerned with Roman literature and Latin Christian poetry and prose. Both sides of the quarrel were based on the works of Aristotle, variously interpreted and developed by Arabic, Greek, and Latin commentators. The differences concerning the principles of the sciences prepared the background of method and of material for Galileo's investigation of motion.

The battle of the *neoterics* in the sixteenth and seventeenth centuries was a battle of rhetoric and of the reduction of other arts to rhetoric. It broadened the province of rhetoric from persuasion in the narrow sense of oratory to include all discourse and communication, prose and poetry, science and art. The two parts of rhetoric—discovery (or invention) and disposition (or proof)—were applied to all disciplines. Plato and Greek literature were studied in the humanities, and the mathematical arts of the quadrivium were elaborated in the sciences. Ramus reformed all the liberal arts and Alsted compiled the first modern encyclopaedia. In this dispute Aristotle was given a bad name, but he was not guilty of as many errors as Cicero and Quintilian.

The battle of the *ancients* and the *moderns* in the seventeenth and eighteenth centuries was a battle of the liberal arts as a whole or a battle of learning. The moderns based their positions on the philosophy of Bacon, Descartes, Newton, or Locke, and they defended modern poetry against ancient poetry. In the humanities, modern as well as classical literature was studied and the new science of philology was used. Indeed, the complexities of the battle are contained in the ambiguities of the word "philology," which is the love of *logos,* or the study of "learning" or of "literature" or of "language." In Martianus Capella's *De nuptiis philologiae et Mercurii* in the fifth century, Mercury represents eloquence, philology "love of learning"; Mercury presents his bride with the seven liberal arts as handmaidens. In Budé's *De philologia* in the sixteenth century, philology is the study of letters or literature. With the instauration of modern philology in the eighteenth and nineteenth century, it became the study of the language of literature. This is the battle treated by Swift. In that battle the Royal Librarian of St. James Library, a classical philologist, is characterized as a "fierce champion of the Moderns."[1] He sometimes lost his head in replacing books on the shelves and put Descartes next to Aristotle and Hobbes next to Plato.[2] In the battle itself, Aristotle shot an arrow at Bacon, whom he missed, but he hit and killed Descartes,[3] much in the manner of the heroes of classical epics.

The last two phases of the battle of the books were so important in the history of American education that it is difficult to account for American education and culture without taking them into account. The programs of the early universities in America were neoteric. The early lists of theses of Harvard College reproduced in Morison's history of Harvard College are neoteric doctrines, and Perry Miller produces evidence to support his contention that the logic of Ramus

[1] *A Tale of a Tub, to which is added The Battle of the Books and the Mechanical Operation of the Spirit,* ed. by A. C. Guthkelch and D. Nichol Smith (Oxford: Oxford University Press, 1920), p. 225.
[2] *Ibid.,* p. 226.
[3] *Ibid.,* pp. 244–245.

was no less influential as a source of Puritanism than the
theology of Augustine and Calvin.[4] The transition from the
revolution of the "neoterics" to the new learning of the "moderns" and the significance of that transition for the arts and
their subject matters may be seen in the education of one man
whose career touched the beginnings of two universities, Dr.
Samuel Johnson, student and tutor in the Connecticut colleges which developed into Yale University and first president
of King's College which developed into Columbia University.

Samuel Johnson received the A.B. at Saybrook College in
1714 at the age of 18. Among his notebooks was one dated
1714 and entitled *Technologia sive technometria; Ars ency-
clopaidia manualis ceu philosophia; Systema liber artis*. Its
preface is a brief (one and a half pages long) history of
philosophy, which ends: "Among these innumerable men the
principal sects were Platonists, Peripatetics, and Eclectics.
The leader of the eclectic sect was that great man Ramus, at
whose feet, as it were, there followed Richardson and then
Ames, the greatest of them, followed him and we follow
Ames. (From all these a new eclectic sect has sprung, *viz.*,
the *Neoterics*.)"[5] The *Technology* or *Encyclopedia* exhibits
several neoteric characteristics that were also notable in the
teaching at Harvard: the interest in encyclopedia and "rule of
encyclopaedia" ("orbis ille et circulus artium," "enkuklios
paedeia," the cycle of learning, or of education, or of culture,
or, as it might also be translated, general education), the
conception of education as *art*, or *techne*, or technology, and
the organization of all knowledge in a series of dichotomous

[4] Morison, *Harvard College in the Seventeenth Century* (Cambridge,
Mass.: Harvard University Press, 1936) Pt. II, pp. 580–638; and Miller *The
New England Mind: The Seventeenth Century* (Boston: Beacon Press,
1961), p. 116.
[5] Preface to *An Encyclopedia of Philosophy*, vol. II of *Samuel Johnson,
President of King's College, His Career and Writings*, ed. Herbert Schneider
and Carol Schneider (New York: Columbia University Press, 1929), p. 61.

The Battle of the Books 181

divisions of the arts. The treatise consists of 1,271 numbered theses, of which the first is the definition of "art" as "the idea representing and directing *eupraxia,*" the ninth a definition of *"eupraxia"* as "the orderly motion or action of an agent in acting," followed by a division of the arts into archetypal and typal, entypal and ectypal, and a classification and treatment of the ectypal arts (which have universal rules and methods) under logic, grammar, rhetoric, arithmetic, geometry, physics (including biology and psychology), and theology. The last four theses are concerned with encyclopedia (the universal and circular comprehension of all the arts), with philosophy (the love of encyclopedia), and with pansophia (the knowledge of all things).

More than fifty years later in his *Autobiography* (1768–70), Johnson complains of the low state of learning in those times. Students had been taught "scholastic cobwebs," and the works of Ramus and Alsted were considered as the highest attainments; "they were not allowed to vary an ace in their thoughts from Dr. Ames' *Medulla Theologiae* and *Cases of Conscience.*" [6] They had heard, in 1714, of "a new philosophy that of late was all in vogue and of such names as Descartes, Boyle, Locke and Newton," but they were cautioned against it as dangerous to religion. No books of learning were available. Johnson lighted accidentally on Bacon's *Advancement of Learning,* remarking parenthetically that it was perhaps the only copy in the country and that nobody knew its value. A well-chosen library was brought to the colony in 1714: it contained Shakespeare and Milton, Locke, Boyle, and Newton. In the ambiguities of the changes recorded by Dr. Johnson, the Neoterics had become scholastics

---

[6] *Autobiography,* vol. I of *Samuel Johnson,* p. 6. In thesis 1,267 of *An Encyclopedia of Philosophy,* he had written fifty years earlier, "See about anything D. R. G. Ames in *Medulla Theologia* and *Cases of Conscience.*"

with the advent of the New Learning. Johnson's pupil, Jonathan Edwards, who was to become third president of the College of New Jersey, later Princeton University, probably learned about Locke from Johnson.

Dr. Johnson continued to revise his work. The influence of Locke's division of the sciences into physica, practica, and semiotice is apparent in the first printed editions of the *Encyclopedia* in 1731, republished and enlarged in 1743 for his Yale students: the division of philosophia, the universe of learning, is into semiotical or rational (logic, grammar, rhetoric, poetry) and real, subdivided into general (or ontology) and particular (physics concerned with creature and theology concerned with creator and our duty). The title of the 1744 edition emphasized the encyclopedic character of philosophy: *An Introduction to the Study of Philosophy, Exhibiting a General View of All the Arts and Sciences.* Johnson became a friend of Bishop Berkeley during his stay in America and corresponded with him about philosophy in 1729–30; Berkeley is quoted in the *Elementa philosophica,* published by Benjamin Franklin in 1752, which was used as a textbook at King's College during the seven years of Johnson's presidency. It opens with definitions of the "circle of learning," "art," "science," "philology," and "philosophy."

"1. Learning (which the Grecians called Cyclopaedia) implies the knowledge of every thing useful to our well-being and true happiness in this life, or our supreme happiness in the life to come. And as our happiness consists in the enjoyment of truth and good, by the right exercise of our understandings, affections, wills and active powers, it must take in every thing that relates both to theory and practice, i.e. both to science and art; for science is the knowledge of truth considered speculatively, and art is the knowledge of truth considered as directive of our practice for the attaining of our true good and happiness. And all the various parts of learning may be reduced to these two, philology, or the study of words and other signs, and philosophy, or the study of the things signified by them." [7] This is familiar ground for later discussion of education: philology "is called also, *Humanity* and the *Belles Lettres,*" philosophy or "the knowledge of things signified together with a practice correspondent thereto" is divided into the study of bodies, or sensible things which constitute the natural world, called physics, and the study of spirits or intelligent moral beings which constitute the moral world, called metaphysics and moral philosophy. [8] The disciplines have become subject matters, and the subject matters have begun the struggle to settle down within the nineteenth- and twentieth-century boundaries of the humanities, the natural sciences, and the social sciences.

The questions raised in the battle of the books were basic and therefore ambiguous questions: neither position in such a controversy is clear or demonstrable, and the old and the new seem to be on both sides of all arguments. Yet the stages and changes of education and learning are determined by positions taken in that controversy because they remove ambiguities to treat unambiguous problems. As controversy, it has been alleged that there has been an antagonism between the humanities and religion, a warfare between science and religion, and a split between the humanities and the sciences. As stages of progress, the humanities, the sciences, and religions have contributed data, methods, and insights to each other, but the meanings of each of the terms and its scope of application change as the progress is traced. Johnson's change from his neoteric position to his espousal of the new

[7] *Ibid.,* vol. II, p. 361.
[8] *Ibid.,* p. 441.

learning may be described in two ways: it may be stated controversially as a discovery that the neoterics were in fact scholastics or ancients; or the two stages may be examined to discover the common marks of modernity which they shared and the differences of problem and circumstance by which the modern becomes ancient in a later modernity.

The old and the new, the ancient and the modern, as their names suggest, have no fixed and absolute marks, but are defined by methods used and subjects treated, under conditioning circumstances and facilitating knowledge, in which ambiguous questions relate matters which are unrelated in the unambiguous answers that are given successively to the questions. It is not a question of the relation of *the* humanities to *the* sciences but a question of the meanings of "humanities" and "sciences" under which the humanities are conceived and developed as sciences, and the sciences are practiced as arts, and sciences and arts are mutually exclusive, in the encyclopedia of learning. In these transitions, the trivial oppositions of the ancients and the moderns contribute to the progress of education. The contribution can be isolated by examining the determination of the ambiguous questions. Johnson's use of "encyclopedia" carries the identifying marks of the neoteric and modern meanings of a critical term or method.

The encyclopedia was involved in the ancient Roman quarrel concerning Greek literature and learning. Some, like Cato, opposed its introduction in Rome, as a debilitating influence; others, like the Scipionic circle, advocated its use as a basis for Roman new greatness. The advocates applied the word *humanitas* to the arts, since "humanity" or "human nature" is understood only by understanding the greatest achievements of man, and in appreciating and advancing those achievements, the liberal arts are a cycle of learning, an *enkuklios paideia*. As in later quarrels, there is an ambiguous touch of modernity and antiquity in both sides; Scipio praises Cato for recognizing that the Roman commonwealth, unlike Greek commonwealths, was based upon the genius, not of one man but of many, and that it was founded, not in one generation, but over a period of several centuries and many ages of men.[9] The mark of the modern, however, is in the "encyclopedia" and interrelation of the arts that permit them to be put to new uses on new subject matters, as in the plea addressed to Cicero himself (in a dialogue written by Cicero) by his brother and his friend to make up for the lack of a history of Rome by applying the art of rhetoric to the writing of history.[10] With the coming of Christianity and in the medieval developments of Judaism and Islam, there were quarrels concerning the use of the pagan arts. The outcome of these controversies is itself a matter of controversy, for the controversies still go on, but there is no doubt that the ancient liberal arts were profoundly modified by the medieval arts or that the preservation of ancient learning is due to the industry and devotion of medieval scribes. The "old logic" in the twelfth century was based on translations of the first two books of Aristotle's *Organon,* the "new logic" on new translations, or newly available translations, of the remaining four books. Logic is an integrated study, however, and writers in the tradition of the old logic made use of the arts of rhetoric and grammar to treat problems that were to be treated otherwise in the new logic. The new logic opened up the problems of the principles of knowledge and proof and led to the opposition of the "ancient logic" and the "modern logic": the ancient logic used the methods of the *Posterior Analytics*

[9] Cicero *De re publica* ii. 1. 2.
[10] Cicero *De legibus* i. 1. 5.–2. 7.

(which were unknown before the coming of the new logic) to base principles on causes and interrelations, while the modern logic used the methods of rhetoric and dialectic or the methods of sophistic and grammar (elaborated from beginnings in the old logic) to base principles on rational agreements or verbal paradoxes.

During the Renaissance the encyclopedia was rediscovered and the liberal arts were revolutionized. The word encyclopedia was used as the name both for programs of education in the liberal arts and for ready reference handbooks of facts and doctrines. There is a natural tendency for a method of discovery to become solidified into a fact or a datum and for commonplaces to cease to be instruments of invention and to become instead topics of iteration and quotation. Peter Ramus and the neoterics used the rhetorical methods of invention and proof to refurbish the encyclopedia of the liberal arts: with success and repetition it became a mechanical method of dichotomous division to order recognized doctrines rather than an inventive method of inquiry concerning new problems. The encyclopedia as organization of knowledge became a classification of branches of knowledge in terms of what was known in each, a dictionary of facts to supplement and correct dictionaries of words. The encyclopedia as program of education became an organization of branches of study in terms of the interrelation of arts of words and of things in the knowledge of all things requisite for acting well.

During the seventeenth and eighteenth centuries the encyclopedia became a universal dictionary of the arts and sciences. It sometimes had a historical organization, as did Moréri's *Le grand dictionnaire historique,* or Hofmann's *Lexicon universale historico-geographico-chronologico-poëtico-philologicum,* and Bayle's *Dictionnaire historique et critique;* it sometimes sought to supplement the new dictionaries of the vulgar tongues by distinguishing between vocabularies that give the significance of words and dictionaries of notions that describe things indicated by words, as did the dictionaries of Furetière, of Corneille, and of Trévoux; it sometimes presented a philosophic basis of the arts and sciences, as did Chauvin's *Lexicon rationale sive thesaurus philosophicus;* it sometimes undertook to explain not only the terms of art but the arts themselves with emphasis on the natural and applied sciences, as did Harris' *Lexicon technicum, or an Universal English Dictionary of Arts and Sciences.* Harris' *Lexicon* was an episode in the seventeenth-century version of the Battle of the Books over the Royal Society and the new sciences. That Battle marks a stage in the separation of the arts from the sciences, and it finds a natural extension in the Battle over modern literature and the new science of philology. When *humanitas* became plural as "the humanities" in the modern languages, the modified term took its meaning not from the nature of man as disclosed in the great achievements of men but from the creative arts and their scientific study, that is, it became a synonym for "beaux arts," "belles lettres," or "philology." The progress of education was by increase in the study of sciences as contrasted to the study of letters, or humanities, or the arts; and the social sciences later developed a scientific method to treat man, humanity, communities, communications, and values. The fragmentation of the subject matter of the arts and sciences continued in the succeeding centuries, and oppositions arose not only from the major distinctions but also between each of the subdivided subjects.

The history of education in the United States has been a history of the Battle of the Books. In the twentieth century the encyclopedia has become general education, *enkuklios paideia.* In the development of general education all the forces that have led to major changes in education at various stages in the past have been operative. In the changed circumstances of the twentieth century they have determined the definition of "general education." The aims of general education have been "general" in four senses adapted to the needs of our times. (1) General education is general in the sense of involving or underlying *all knowledge.* There has been an evolution from the survey courses of the 1920's, which covered all knowledge, to the general courses of the present, which examine and use methods to solve problems of explanation and action and to bind knowledge together. In that evolution, disciplines have tended to become arts to be practiced rather than fields to be mastered. (2) General education is general in the sense of providing the means of communication and bases of community to *all men.* As the "new men" of Rome were agents in the preparation for world empire, the "new men" of the twentieth century are agents with new possibilities of action because of changed world relations resulting from economic, social, and political revolutions. The art of resolving problems by discussion, rather than by expert or authoritative knowledge, constitutes the general education in public affairs requisite for the preservation of democratic communities and the formation of a world community under the rule of law. There has been an evolution in general education from inculcation of the arts by which men get what they want to the formation of a conception of democracy as the use of reason to come to agreement by discussion. (3) General education is general in the sense of forming a framework to organize *all experiences* of individual men. It is education for character, which is a second nature, formed to realize the potentialities of human nature in accordance with free choice and right reason. The evolution from subject matter and information to discipline and discussion has been accompanied by an evolution in the education of the whole man from harmonizing preferences and passions to ordering powers and actions. (4) General education is general in the sense of building on the values of *all cultures* and traditions of the world. Our approach to knowledge of other peoples has evolved since the Second World War from an area-language descriptive communication based on images which peoples construct of each other to an examination of common problems faced by the members of a world community, and from the divisive confrontation of Greco-Roman, Judeo-Christian, Islamic, Hindu, Chinese, and other traditions to the integrative interplay among the opportunities of one world.

The disputes concerning general education have been continuations of the Battle of the Books. The Neoterics or Moderns have continued to defend the encyclopedia and to advocate liberal education as the liberal arts and as general education. The moderns in general education have identified new problems and have experimented with new methods for their solution. General education has been learning and teaching new disciplines and new arts adapted to the recognition and solution of new problems. The Paleoterics or Traditionalists have sought to return subjects that were parts of liberal education at its last stage to the effectiveness which they once had. They defend training in the liberal arts and therefore advocate liberal education but not general education. Liberal education is the acquisition of the knowledge and methods of particular subject matters, taught by experts in those fields, who can bring creative insight to imparting skills and knowledge in particular subject matters. The approach is interdisciplinary, but it is an approach to subjects, and traditionalists tend to be dubious about the general or the universal.

As in the earlier battles, the oppositions are sharply stated antagonistic differences; when stated fairly in their own terms, as in the preceding paragraph, they tend to seem trivial or reconcilable differences of emphasis. Both sides recognize the need of innovation and tradition; both use the past to solve the problems of the present. Yet, despite such likenesses in the opposed positions, the resolution of this battle will lead, like the resolution of past battles, to a new form of education, and the new form that uses the past to form new disciplines will differ from the new form that uses the past to rehabilitate established or accepted disciplines. The neoterics must go on to a new form of education: they cannot return to the philosophy of Greece, the liberal arts of Rome or the Middle Ages or the Renaissance, or even to the general education of the Hutchins college of twenty-five years ago. The traditionalists must go back to the liberal education of experts teaching what they know with confidence and creativity: it cannot be a development of general education in which a structure of problems and methods is used to prepare all students to recognize and face the novelties of thought, action, and experience in the modern world, and in which instructors adapt their teaching to a common pattern rather than teaching what they please as they please. There is talk of pluralism and universality in both camps. The one is a pluralism of disciplines to treat common problems; the other is a pluralism of fields and of approaches that experts think proper to different fields. The one is a universality or commonality of inclusiveness and connection; the other is a universality or commonality of distribution and selection. To bring out the differences, it is wise to abandon the effort to state both sides fairly in their own terms and to set forth instead a statement of the issues as viewed by the neoterics, who continue the tradition of Ramism and the New Learning in American education, but abandon the specific forms of those traditions to traditionalists.

As in the past, it is not possible to distinguish a neoteric from a traditionalist by determining whether he reads and teaches ancient or modern books. The influence of the neoterics in the transition from medieval to modern education was to reformulate the liberal arts for the study of Greek literature and modern literatures and for the study of ancient mathematics, medicine and cosmology, and modern sciences. Bentley was a modern in the seventeenth and eighteenth centuries; he was one of the inventors of the new methods of classical philology. The neoteric innovations at the University of Chicago have sometimes been called "Aristotelian," and I was somewhat surprised to discover, after I had come to the University of Chicago, that I too was an Aristotelian. It might seem that an Aristotelian philosophy, an Aristotelian literary criticism, and an Aristotelian general education are traditionalist. As they emerge in the long line of neoteric and modern encyclopedias and programs of study in American education, however, they are clearly neoteric, and they may be used as starting points for new forms of philosophy, criticism, and education.

I have always been a neoteric. From the beginning of my teaching career I have worked with committees and staffs forming and teaching general education courses. Even my interest in Aristotle was a neoteric discovery. During many years of undergraduate and graduate study at Columbia University and the University of Paris, I never took a course on Aristotle because none was given at those universities in those years. I had many courses on Plato in which I learned that he dichotomized the world into two worlds of changeless ideas and changing things, and that Socrates played sophistical tricks on his adversaries. I had also learned that Aristotle had enslaved men's minds for two thousand years. When I read Aristotle I found the experience interesting and rewarding, and therefore I gave courses on Aristotle, edited collections of the works of Aristotle, and wrote papers on philosophic problems that he treated and on the methods he used in stating and solving them. I was amazed to be called an Aristotelian for two reasons. In the first place, my interpretation of Aristotle does not agree with what is commonly held, on the authority of recent scholars, to be Aristotelian doctrines and errors. In the second place, the positions I have taken on many philosophical problems are not the positions I have attributed to Aristotle, and the methods by which I have discussed the issues and established my conclusions are different from those I attributed to Aristotle in important respects. I have never troubled to point these differences out because the name "Aristotelian" is used not to describe a person or a position but to be unkind, and if I was to be charged with guilt by association, I could not do better than be associated with the Master of Them that Know.

Several of my colleagues at the University of Chicago and I published a collaborative work, *Critics and Criticism, Ancient and Modern* (Chicago: University of Chicago Press, 1952). Battles were recounted in the work, but they were not battles between the ancients and the moderns, despite their appearance in the title. It was a neoteric pluralistic work. One of the approaches that we made to criticism was based on Aristotle's *Poetics* which we held, perhaps somewhat arrogantly, had never been interpreted correctly or used effectively in the period of almost twenty-four hundred years since its composition. Our uses of other approaches and our expositions of the advantages of pluralism were barely noticed. The position of the "Chicago School" was Aristotelian. We were convinced that the treatment of a work of art as an artificial object to be examined in itself brought important properites of the work of art to attention and heightened appreciation of it. None of our critics criticized our novel approach to Aristotle. The method was assumed to be Aristotle's, possibly because we acknowledged that it was; it was assumed that it was not a good method of criticism, possibly because it was ancient. The neoteric approach is to discover the new and the stimulating even in the familiar and the forgotten. We were not being pluralistic in the sense of reporting that one can approach poetry in this way, in that way, and in still other ways. We viewed the appreciation of poetry as a complex experience, and we sought to bring out different aspects of that experience in criticism. We were not practicing eclecticism but applying esthetics: there are wrong as well as pertinent ways of philosophizing, but among the wrong ways the one which operates on the assumption that there is one right way which is recognized easily by the meanings it sets forth and the nonsense it detects in all other approaches is more prolific of errors and stultifications than most other misused methods or misguided assumptions.

During the thirty years of the evolution of the general education program at the University of Chicago, I learned repeatedly during visits to New York and Washington, Boston and New Haven (opinions were less uniform in the West than in the East) that the general education programs were Aristotelian in Chicago. I never knew how to relate that judgment to what we were doing or what we were saying. I knew no Aristotelians, in the sense of men who adhered to the principles, methods, and doctrines of Aristotle, among my colleagues. In my own contributions I have borrowed more from Dewey than from Aristotle, but the common borrowing may still have been "Aristotelian" since I am convinced that Dewey shares much with Aristotle if account is taken of appropriate neoteric transformations of a common method to changed circumstances. Moreover, we did borrow from the language and distinctions of Aristotle in constructing the encyclopedia essential to neoteric education, and we were convinced that metaphysics provides the basis for that encyclopedia and for the higher learning in America. The Ramist encyclopedia, which influenced early American education and gave form to Alsted's and Commenius' compilations of knowledge, had moved from the arts of discovery to the recitation of discoveries. The encyclopedia of the new learning based on Bacon and Locke, which influenced American education in the eighteenth and nineteenth centuries and gave form to the French *Encyclopédie,* had moved from the augmentation of knowledge to the subdivision of the branches of knowledge. In the face of the resultant fragmentation of knowledge, the new encyclopedia should bring out the connections among the branches of knowledge and should make the methods used to form and connect them available in general education. It is possible that a single method may be adapted to the unification of all sciences and all knowledge, but a pluralism of methods, disciplines, and arts is better adapted to the neoteric orientation to new problems, new situations, and new discoveries. General education based on the methods of the natural sciences, the social sciences, and the humanities may with justification be viewed as an adaptation of Aristotle's distinction of the theoretic, practical, and poetic sciences. More important than establishing the remote ancestry of the program is recognition of the fact that it has grown and changed constantly, and neoterics may hope that changes made today will build on past accomplishments to go on to a new program. It would be disastrous if a traditionalist abandonment of general education brought us back to a program indistinguishable from the requirements and distributions of the 1920 or the 1892 form of liberal education.

The forces of our times make for neotericism as did the forces operative in Ancient Rome and in Renaissance Europe. The basic force is the appearance of "new men" everywhere, and the education proper to the new men of the present is determined by the contacts of cultures, in which humanity or mankind emerges in a new normative and effective form while the individual or man faces new possibilities and new dilemmas. One of the first actions of the government of India after its establishment in 1947 was to appoint a University Education Commission in 1948 under the chairmanship of Radhakrishnan. The report of the Commission, published in 1950, contains an excellent statement of "The Aims of University Education" [11] based on the five objectives set forth in the Draft Constitution of the Republic of India adopted in August, 1949. The problems of educational theory and practice are taken up under the five heads of democracy, justice, liberty, equality, and fraternity.[12] "Professional education is different from general education, not so much in its subject matter as in its method, outlook and objective. To give a basic understanding of the principles of science, history and literature is the aim of the general course; to train experts in them is the aim of the specialized course." [13] The treatment of general education in chapter V [14] makes use of the American experience in general education.[15] A committee of Indian educators visited the United States in 1954 to study the forms that general education had taken in the United States. A second team came in 1956. The representatives of seven American universities went to India in 1957 to continue the

[11] *The Report of the University Education Commission, December 1948– August 1949* (Delhi: published by the Manager of Publications, 1950), I, 32–67.
[12] *Ibid.*, p. 36.
[13] *Ibid.*, p. 42.
[14] *Ibid.*, pp. 117–38.
[15] *Ibid.*, p. 121.

discussion and to help Indian universities develop general education.

The emergence of new men in Europe and in the Americas stimulated general education in long established educational systems as well as in newly formed colleges and universities. In 1957 the French Office of Higher Education invited the four American Research Councils—the American Council of Learned Societies, the National Research Council, the Social Science Research Council, and the National Council of Education—to send two representatives each to meet in discussion of problems of general education with a like number of French educators representing the disciplines of the humanities, the natural sciences, the social sciences, and education. The committee of eight then went to Norway to hold a like conference in Oslo. The problems of general education that had arisen in France and Norway were consequences of changed conditions. In both countries students with approximately the same background and training had for a long time sought entrance to universities and technical schools in fairly constant or moderately increasing numbers. What should be done when greatly increased numbers from more diversified backgrounds sought higher education? What is general education for all citizens? How should the new kind of students be given some acquaintance with and some competence in all knowledge? What is a unified experience in education and how should education contribute to the formation of character? The rapidly expanding University of Puerto Rico set up a separate undergraduate Faculty of General Studies for variations of like reasons. In the United States the problem of general education has arisen, as it has more recently in India, from phases of the relation of technical or professional education to the broader and more basic aims of education: the fear that the land-grant colleges might debase academic standards by emphasizing technology and agriculture early earned them the name "cow colleges"; the new junior colleges, community colleges, and the old teachers colleges transformed into liberal arts colleges have recently developed in a cloud of controversy about their experimental contributions to general education and their susceptibility to local pressures or their abandonment of education for vocational and community training.

The programs of general education for new men in new conditions are affected by new influences in the proliferation of knowledge, the contacts of cultures, growing awareness of mankind and world community, and new problems in the formation of the individual and the integration of character. New methods of teaching fundamental disciplines and making available the ideas and the methods developed in the various branches of human knowledge and activity provide the basis for new encyclopedias and new synoptic programs of studies. A sense of the importance of understanding the values of other cultures and promoting communication among the peoples of the world has broken the rigidity of divisive cultural traditions. Humanity in the sense of a common awareness of mankind has prepared a reorientation from the differences of the humanities and the sciences to a search for common solutions to common problems despite differences of cultural traditions, ideological beliefs, and local loyalties. The recognition that education is an activity and a practice of the arts of living has reduced the artificial separation of reason, attitude, and feeling in translating the methods of knowing, doing, and making into a general education for the formation of character.

The University of Chicago has made important contributions to general education: it has promoted the adaptation of the encyclopedia and the disciplines of learning to the problems of men knowing, deliberating, and perceiving. The changes in the program that are now under consideration are one more stage in the Battle of the Books. How can the new program recast the disciplines that have been the continuing strength of general education to equip men to take hold of new possibilities and to face new problems? There are many ways to treat the structure of problems and methods of the modern world. One will be formed and put into effect as a result of discussion and agreement at the University of Chicago during the next few months. It would be unwise to predict the outcome, since the future is uncertain; and it would be imprudent to advertise my preferences, since I shall be a participant in the deliberations, and foreknown positions seldom survive to the end in the dialectic of discussion. On the other hand, the general lines of the Battle of the Books in which we are engaged are clear, and the possible courses of action should be seen concretely. To avoid the restrictive vagueness of cautionary abstraction I suggest that we abandon the perspective of faculty program construction for the perspective of student educational planning. Imagine a student who came to the university about twenty-five years ago. When he was ready to graduate, the A.B. was the degree for general education, and he had passed fourteen comprehensive examinations to qualify for it. He is now planning an education for his son and daughter. Since he is a neoteric he is convinced that new disciplines, different from those he acquired, are now needed, and that those new disciplines will not correspond to the four subject matter divisions of the graduate school. He is also convinced that the new disciplines will be based on the old disciplines but will avoid the rigidities and limitations into which they had fallen, and that the liberal arts will preserve the continuity that contributed to their effectiveness when they were adapted to new problems and circumstances in past renaissances and revolutions in education. His meditation is therefore a neoteric revolution of four general courses to fit a new encyclopedia or cycle of learning. It runs as follows:

"I had a good course in the humanities in which I acquired arts of appreciation, analysis, and criticism. It did not extend beyond the fine arts, but I learned to read books—history, philosophy, rhetoric, drama, epic, prose fiction, lyric poetry. I hope that the disciplines have been extended now to include the reading and interpretation of works of science, law, and policy as well. The humanities are the study of the great achievements of man. It was an accident of history that they were limited in modern times to the fine arts. The works of Euclid, Newton, and Adam Smith have humanistic aspects; poetry, music, and mathematics have comparable structures, and tropes, analogies, and proportions are basically the same; my understanding of plot as the argument of drama was improved by studying related arguments of orators and related facts of history, and I should have liked to extend that understanding further by relating those structures of discourse to the structures of arguments in philosophical and scientific inquiry and proof. The humanities ought to become again not a study of philology or the language of the arts but a study of the arts themselves in which the manner of presentation is related to what is presented. Philosophy belongs in the humanities because it is the art of arts and the science of sciences, and arts are practiced in the discovery and transmission of the sciences.

"I had a good course in the social sciences in which I learned about the behavior of individuals and communities, about character, action, and institutions. The disciplines of the behavioral sciences had already been extended to include intellectual and cultural behavior. But there was a tendency to explain away philosophy and science, morals and justice, art and taste by social circumstances, mores, and ideology. I hope that the reciprocity of the humanities and the social sciences has become more apparent as they come to be seen as arts of making and practices of doing rather than as independent and contrasted subject matters to which antagonistic methods are appropriate. They will then be related as architectonic disciplines, for the arts or human sciences are architectonic because man's great accomplishments in all fields are accomplishments of the arts he has acquired, and the practical or social sciences are architectonic because men's characters, values, and accomplishments are conditioned by the social and cultural circumstances in which they are reared and by the attitudes, available materials, and sanctions that determine their common activities. Behavior and community affect interests and criteria in art, science, and philosophy; art, science, and philosophy are behavior affecting men and communities. In antiquity, Aristotle thought of political science as a single science with two parts: politics concerned with the institutions of states and ethics concerned with the habits of men; economics was a prerequisite to politics and the intellectual virtues—including art, prudence, and science —were treated in ethics. In the eighteenth century political economy was a single science, and in the twentieth century the sociology of knowledge is restrained in its imperialistic tendencies by the philosophies of sociology. We have been developing new architectonic disciplines in the social sciences.

"I had a good course on the nature of the physical world, including the natural functions and evolution of animate beings. I hope that the disciplines of the natural sciences have been extended to reconstitute natural philosophy to acquaint students with the interplay of ideas and methods that relate the particles of quantum mechanics to the cosmos of relativity physics, the changes in mathematics that have made possible and have resulted from changes in physics to the changes in knowledge which they embodied and produced, and the use of models and explanations in the whole intermediate region. I hope that the disciplines of natural philosophy are extended to include the bearing of the nature of things on the values and the activities and the communities of men and to the influence of the concepts and methods of science on other disciplines. World order has a meaning in the social sciences as well as in the natural sciences, and the institution of world order by the one science and the discovery of world order by the other science are not unrelated to the world order exemplified in practice of the arts of humanity or mankind. Natural philosophy is an architectonic discipline that influences and is influenced by the practice of the architectonic disciplines of arts and of practical actions.

"In each of these three courses I was taught to use disciplines that cut across the subject matters of the humanities, the social sciences, and the natural sciences. That was an essential aspect of general education, and the changes that I suppose have occurred make the scope and importance of the disciplines clearer and depart from the supposition that they are applied to distinct and separate subject matters. I also took two courses that integrated the knowledge presented in the other courses—the History of Western Civilization, and Observation, Interpretation, and Integration (which later became the Organization, Methods, and Principles of Knowledge). I hesitate to speculate on the new form that the discipline of history and the discipline of theory-formation might take, but provision should be made for the disciplines by which historical facts are determined and theoretic laws are formulated, and in which the student is made familiar with important facts and ideas of history and with basic structures of phenomena and conception. They should both treat facts and communications, ideas and facts, words and actions, and the interpretation and explanation of statements and activities. We live in a world of concrete facts, which are recounted in history once they have occurred, and which are observed, interpreted, and integrated as they occur and after they occur, to be projected in statements and actions based on history and theory designed to determine facts when the future becomes the present."

Our imaginary student did not go beyond the A.B. degree in his formal education, but he had received a general education and he has continued to use it. His plan was thought out hastily, and it did not have the benefit of expert academic debate and refinement. But he is a neoteric and a pluralist, and he realizes that the structure of problems and methods which he seeks is an encyclopedia that may be made a program of teaching and learning in other courses than those which he has constructed. What is important is that education should acquaint men with such problems and methods, and I share our student's confidence that it can be done better by planning the structure than by waiting for its emergence from the accidental joining of particular skills and individual collections of facts and information.

THE ROLE OF A LIBERAL ARTS COLLEGE WITHIN A UNIVERSITY

Edward H. Levi

In summary, the role of a liberal arts college within a university is to be a genuine part of that university, giving and responding to the other parts. Under fortunate circumstances, the college adds greatly to the university's conception of an intellectual and cultural community. The introduction of many minds into many fields of learning along a broad spectrum keeps alive questions about the accessibility, if not the unity, of knowledge. The choices made by those who are not fully committed measure the uses of scholarship, and emphasize the relationship between scholarship and practical action and the importance of contemplation and understanding. These choices encourage a reappraisal of the accustomed routine. Along the way the community has gained in interest and liveliness. The university is strengthened as an institution guiding its own growth through the persistence of questions even when the questions do not arise from the inner logic of a protected subject matter. If the college's persistence in asking "What knowledge is worth having?" creates tension or distraction—and it does—the established order on balance can nevertheless be well pleased. For the drama of the college, and a compelling drama it is, is the miraculous transformation of the bright and untutored into minds of greater power through the victory of the disciplines. But it is a victory that knows no loser, and a transformation that works its change upon the disciplines themselves.

This is an idealized account that fails to stress many of the important characteristics, problems, and paradoxes of the

modern university of which the college is a part. It is difficult
to describe the modern university. It is apt to be large and
complicated. It is hard, in any event, to be objective about
one's environment and companions. Generalized descriptions
may miss the mark. The balance within one institution between undergraduate and graduate teaching, research, the
carrying on of the liberal arts tradition at all levels, including
the graduate and the professional, and the assumption of
responsibilities and service functions may be quite different
from that at another. But certain points can be made, if not
for all, at least for this one.

To begin with, the range of activities is enormous. It
should not be necessary to make this point about the institution which had the first self-sustaining atomic pile, which man-
ages the Argonne National Laboratory, and which has, as an
integral part of its concern, hospitals where decisions of life
are made every day. The range goes from nursery schools to
postdoctoral training and guidance for the professions, the
development of the most intricate of laboratories, the operation of educational enterprises in Asia and Latin America,
the creation of some of the most significant centers in the
world for the study of non-Western cultures. There still may
be some popular belief that a university is mainly an institution to which the young are sent with the hope that they will
not be too visible while they are growing up. But in general
the community at large knows, and perhaps knows too well,
that the research and actions of the universities are often
pivotal to national security, public health and order, economic and industrial development, and that the understanding of other societies which may be achieved here may
determine our ability to shape a peaceful world with them.

Usefulness has invited burdens. Necessity has compelled
their acceptance. We are an urban university. Because the

cities, states, and federal government have not solved the problems of urban blight and urban living, the universities within the cities have become instrumentalities for redevelopment. Our campus plan becomes the means for achieving a community plan. Our conception of the university has undergone a radical change. The university is no longer an island separated from a community. There is a sense in which the community has become part of the university, imposing upon the institution the requirements that in this new relationship it avoid officiousness and the assumption of powers which it does not have, on the one hand, and on the other, that as lines of autonomy fade the institution preserve its own identity.

The range of activities and the assumption of new responsibilities impose great burdens upon the institution. Even without these burdens a university would not meet the tests imposed by a moderately responsible management expert. Most universities are not planned in the sense necessary either for a business venture or a centrally controlled eleemosynary institution. And this university is planned less than most. The management of the University of Chicago, while ultimately in the hands of the Board of Trustees, in large part resides within the faculty, organized into a federal system of ruling bodies of divisions, schools, and the college, with sub-ruling bodies of departments, collegiate divisions, institutes, centers and committees, and an over-all council. But the most important ruling body in this structure, with the greatest power and freedom, and upon whom everything else depends, is the individual professor. The gentlemen who invented the phrase "administration," or, worse still, "central administration," as applied to the University of Chicago, were either unfamiliar with the university, or possessors of a great sense of humor. Yet somehow there is sufficient coherence to marshal and still not interfere with energy and creativity. This fact is recognized by industrial firms when they praise their own laboratories as having the freedom of a university. Three factors are involved. The first is the self-selection of the faculty, whose standards and abilities derive in part from the kind of education you are receiving. The second is the impetus of the character of the institution itself, including a recognition that the system will work only with a minimum of rules and regulations. And third, through discussions more or less rational at many levels, and through ceremonies of many different kinds, the institution each day rediscovers and informally redirects its aims. This kind of self-planning, which is so important to the spirit of this institution, is not easy to achieve, but is much more compelling than may be at first recognized, and it is a priceless asset worth preserving. In these matters Chicago is aided by its comparative small-ness in numbers and by its location in a living as well as a working community. In a sense there is no such thing as "after hours" at this university.

It is against this kind of background that the role of the liberal arts college at Chicago must be examined. The college is not alone. It is a part among many. It is a most important part. It is entitled to regard itself in the same way most of the divisions and schools regard themselves, as the heart of the university. It is not in the Chicago tradition to be bashful in such matters, nor should we be. Happily our college has an appropriate sense of mission. This sets it apart from the undergraduate schools of some universities, which have lost the sense of identity and purpose once achieved by the early liberal arts colleges when they were training schools to elevate the spirits and manners of future gentlemen through the civilizing influences of the humanities, or when they were professional schools for the noble vocation of the ministry.

In having a sense of mission, our college joins other portions of the university that also have an enormous sense of dedication and purpose. Our college is or should be concerned with the effects of a total educational process upon the student. This concern is shared by many of the professional schools. Of course our college is concerned with separating out the important from the trivial, and of using ideas to give meaning to facts. But this is true, or should be, through the entire university. It does not diminish the importance of the college to say that it is in good company, even though the missionary may be happiest when among the infidels.

What then gives to the college a unique role within the university? Although it also shares this function with other areas, more than any other area the college is the means for introducing the student to the university and to new subject matters. At a superficial level this means there is a time for testing and discovery to find out what the institution regards as important and to learn whether the descriptions and slogans given by the mass media to describe college life—the brilliance and maturity of the students, the indifference of the faculty, the prevalence of large lecture classes, the use of graduate students as teachers, the rules of the administration, such as "publish or perish"—are really correct. Over the country, a whole new class of professional personnel of assistant deans of students and advisors has arisen to mediate between the students and their institutions. The observations of these new professionals given in addresses at annual meetings of demi-learned societies, and apparently on any other occasion when they are allowed to speak, would confirm the worst fears that colleges are not primarily concerned with intellectual matters. The college student comes from and into a subsidized world. It is not clear to him where the subsidy begins or stops, and a subsidy presumably means that the institution has a high regard for the purpose of the subsidy. In this setting the hotel functions of the institution, the regulations of dormitory life, the location of residence halls, and the conditions of the food—always horrible—are given high priority. But these matters perhaps are really not as important as the opportunity given to the college to introduce students to the fields or structures of knowledge.

As you undoubtedly know, contrary to what is the general impression, many faculty prefer teaching undergraduates. They say that for some reason undergraduates are brighter and more intellectually responsive. I doubt whether undergraduates are brighter. Most of them become graduate students, and it is doubtful that their wit has been dulled so quickly by old age, particularly since one can see that same wit and responsiveness during the first year of a professional school. The excitement and brightness arise, I think, because of the willingness of the uncommitted mind (and uncommitted is not quite the right term—unroutinized may be better) if sufficiently challenged, to test the boundaries that convention has laid down. The result can be a partnership between faculty and student in which the faculty member is also challenged to try to point a path through a subject matter, or to exemplify that subject matter in the more careful view of a particular situation. This kind of movement through a discipline becomes a demonstration in intellectual honesty—a demonstration that only makes its point when there is the sudden realization that intellectual purity is not naturally within any of us. It may be, if the subject allows, that students and faculty together can explore the uncertain area of the application of competing general principles for purposes of practical decision—an essential kind of training for the citizen and very much in the liberal arts tradition. A college thus can become a generalizing influence within the institution, a way of communication among the disciplines, a way of restating advances of knowledge in the simplest terms, which may be the most difficult and significant terms, and a way of thinking through problem areas, with the advantage of seeing the same problem change its content and meaning as it is handled by different disciplines. I have used the term "generalization," but I have also been willing to link it to the handling of a very specific subject matter. I am reminded—and, of course, it is only an analogy —of a quotation from Giacometti, commenting on the fear of many artists of painting from nature, because the painting, if realistic, would be labeled unoriginal and banal. "Actually," he said, "it's just the other way around. The closer you stick to what you *really* see the more astonishing your work will be. Reality isn't unoriginal, it's just unknown." The question, of course, is what you see, and one can see the larger in the more detailed.

I have mentioned the sense of mission that the college has. I do not believe the college can be a viable set of communities within the university without that sense of mission. The college has had an important past and a tradition of effort that has influenced undergraduate education throughout the country. There was a time when this was a monolithic program, ideally set to occur from the third year of high school through the second year of college. For various reasons, some of them accidental, this dramatic reshaping of the national pattern of the high school–college years did not occur. Instead there has been a continued upgrading of high school education. It might be possible, indeed, perhaps by lengthening the present high school programs by one year, to place the burden of the liberal arts curriculum upon them and to have the universities retreat into what would then be termed specialized or graduate programs. But this would deprive the universities of the coordinating, simplifying, and

210 Edward H. Levi

searching influence of a first-rate college program. Our college has had a brilliant past. We should build upon it. But we must recognize that in the context of the present developed structure of education, the road home is not back. We must build upon the qualities we have. This university has always been proud of its interdisciplinary character, and of its tradition of continuing and inquiring discussion that made Whitehead once describe the university as the nearest example in the modern world to ancient Athens. This was a long time ago, but we have not forgotten it. It is a tradition worth preserving. It is a tradition that the college can claim for itself. The strength of that sense of mission and tradition is exemplified by the naturalness with which this present series of discussions and seminars arose.

If the college finds its mission and its role within the university in this unifying and inquiring function, the college will gain the strength to fulfill this task only if the members of the faculties within the university are in fact willing to engage in undergraduate teaching in sufficient numbers. Four of the present collegiate divisions are based not only upon that organization of knowledge which has made possible the present general education courses, but on the structure beyond the departments for graduate work. The collegiate divisions thus will provide another opportunity to see whether in any meaningful way scholars in related areas find it worthwhile to develop a common or parallel treatment of subject matter. The colleges should help greatly in the development of coordinated programs at the more specialized level where these programs of necessity will go beyond departmental boundaries. For some of these tasks there is no doubt the divisional and college faculties will respond. They have already done so in great numbers. I hasten to add that I think it is a great mistake to assume that the only course worthwhile must be interdepartmental, interdisciplinary, or in some way integrating or coordinating. The fact is, however, that for many departments, courses that may meet the standards of the present general education programs can be of great help in establishing interdepartmental relationships which over time can result in much greater strength for a combined area, or which within a department can help exemplify its very principle of organization. The courses in non-Western civilization are a good example of the first; a sequence in the geophysical sciences would be an example of the latter. In my own judgment the distinction between general education courses as liberal arts courses, on the one hand, and specialized courses as non-liberal but graduate on the other, has been stultifying to the college and to the divisions. It avoids the major aspect of one basic problem of undergraduate education today, the necessity to see and develop specialized courses so that they do indeed reflect the astonishing wonders of reality within a larger intellectual setting. The failure to develop such courses ultimately will result in the failure of the general education courses as well.

The organization of the college into separate colleges under the direction and coordination of the dean and the college council will not work if these colleges do not in fact become communities with something of an existence of their own. They must become areas where communication is established between faculty and students, where ceremonies and events reaffirm the ideals of the community, and where the concern of the faculty, which is actually easily aroused, for the education of their students will give rise to those informal pressures that guide and induce faculty participation. The colleges must take hold to help develop educational and cultural programs that are outside the curriculum, and that do not take the form of courses or any formal work, but nevertheless, or perhaps on that account, can add immeasurably to the life of the students.

It has been one of the interesting attributes of the university to confuse curriculum planning and structural arrangements with more basic questions dealing with knowledge itself or with the aims of education. Of course, the curriculum and the structural arrangements must serve the aims of education; to think of the curriculum and the structure as ends in themselves, or somehow symbolic of the structure of knowledge itself, has given too much rigidity to both curriculum and structure, and has discouraged consideration and discussion or more important matters. The need at the college level is to have the educational mechanisms responsive to the tension between the impossibility of knowing everything and the need to know enough, between the demands of one field and the importance of knowing others, between the craftsmanship of the specialist and the conversion of insights gained from the specific into the more general. The college organization should operate to help confront the participants with these problems, encouraging new solutions, inviting new participants, and thus in itself facilitating the process whereby both general and specific education can become liberal.

As I understand it, this is the theory of the college program at the University of Chicago. It is good to know that the voices of the College are strong and many, joining in that diversity and unity which gives the college its special place.

Printed and bound by CPI Group (UK) Ltd, Croydon, CR0 4YY

09/06/2025

14685709-0001